Additional works by Richard Proctor

These books can be found and acquired at:
    BathroomEconomics.com

Liberty: Will it Survive the 21st Century?
    A 6 Volume Set

Bathroom Economics
    An easily read economics book.

Easily Understood Economics
    Especially good for high school homeschooling.

Saving the Constitution
    A paragraph by paragraph explanation of the
        original Constitution of 1787 in today's English.

A Constitution If You Can Keep It
    Written for the high school level student.
    It explains the Constitution of 1787 with
    questions and answers.

Advanced educational opportunities

Provis Institute of Political Economics
    An educational institution found at provisinstitute.com
    This institute teaches economics as Adam Smith
        meant it to be.
    Undergraduate and graduate degrees can be earned at a
        reasonable cost that anyone can afford.
    All Books can also be acquired on this site.

Bathroom Economics

Richard D. Proctor PhD

Published by:
Provis Press
Kaysville, UT 84037
Provis@sulmega.com
801-719-6291

ISBN: 978-0-578-21333-0

Published in the United States of America

Cover by Brian Twede

CONTENTS

Preface

Our Current Situation

It is sad but true, our nation has almost no understanding of what liberty means. Since the early 1960s our citizens have never been taught anything that would enable them to understand what liberty really is and the financial effects of what the politicians are doing. I wrote the statement below around 2005, and it is still as true as it was then, maybe even more so.

There is nothing in our society that we know less about, that affects our lives more profoundly than economics. And politicians use this fact constantly to control our lives and to get votes based on false information and ideas.

We are led like lambs to the slaughter because by and large we don't understand any better than the lambs what is happening.

That statement is the core of the purpose of *Bathroom Economics* – which is to help you better understand what is happening. You can't fight against something you know nothing about. As individuals begin to understand what is happening they will rise to the occasion.

Introduction and Government Economics

Our economic lives depend on our understanding of economics, including such basic items as what we spend for bread and milk, the interest rates on our savings accounts, how much we spend for a car, and what kind of a life we will have during retirement. Do we want to leave these items to other people to determine for us?

We work our entire lives and carefully invest in our future and then discover the value has been lost over time and wonder what we can do about it, but we seldom take the time to learn the concepts that govern our future. Shouldn't we take the time to learn why prices go up and interest rates change? Aren't these items just as important to us as how we earn our living? Isn't it as important to keep our earnings and savings as it was to earn them in the first place?

Economics is a study of how to understand the causes and effects on our earnings and savings for retirement. I believe that keeping what we have earned is as important as earning it in the first place.

Do you think that the politicians care whether or not you keep your earnings or do they mostly care whether or not they keep their jobs? If the American citizens understood these principles, do you think it is possible that the politicians would act differently?

What Is Economics?

Think about this: how many of you have had a class in basic mathematics? Then consider how many had a class in basic economics. Why did so few have classes in economics? Isn't it equally important? Now think about this: do all math teachers teach the same concepts? Of course they do. Addition and subtraction are always the same.

Now do all economics professors teach the same principles? No. Not only do the economics professors not all teach the same principles, often they teach completely opposing concepts. Why the difference?

Economics deals with the distribution of scarce resources, goods, and services among competing wants. A good, service, or resource can become scarce because there isn't enough of the item available or because too much of the item is wanted; it then becomes a study of how people deal with scarcity.

In other words, do you have everything that you want? Well, if you don't do your friends and acquaintances have everything they want? No. Nobody has everything they want and that creates scarcity and everything is scarce in one way or another.

The buying and selling of goods and services takes place in the market or marketplace. A market or marketplace for a good or service is anywhere that good or service is bought or sold. The marketplace is huge, so to reach some reasonable conclusions, the economist must do something to make the marketplace into a smaller size.

Creating models is a method of doing this. Models are not mysterious or difficult. You find them in all parts of your life. Models are created by making assumptions about many variables and then limiting these variables so they can be easily managed. After a model is created, additional factors are slowly added to analyze what their individual effects are.

Consider an item that is produced in Brazil, Chile, or China. It should be next to impossible to buy it here in the United States at a good price, right? It obviously has to be shipped thousands of miles, and that must be expensive. This book will discuss how things can be available for you to purchase easily, even though they are scarce and are produced on the other side of the world.

Another major part of this book will be to consider what the price should be and how it is determined. Remember everybody involved in getting the product to you. It must include the manufacturer or producer of the product, and the trucking firm that gets the product to the warehouse. We must also consider the transportation and the handling to get it on a plane or ship or train or truck. The costs of the plane or ship or train or truck, and the next warehouse where it is delivered by the plane or train or ship or truck. Also, the transportation to the retail store by train or truck must be considered along with the profit of the retail store where you purchase the item. All of these businesses must be paid for their time and their equipment and must all make a profit and all of these profits and expenses must be included in the price that you finally pay.

10

With all of these costs everything at the store must cost hundreds of dollars, right? Why celery from Chile must cost at least $10 or $20 or many even $50 per stalk. Think about the huge number of people who have combined together to give you the opportunity to have a stalk of celery from Chile, and of course, they are all expecting payment for their services. All of these people want you to have this stalk of celery, and they don't even know you. WHAT A SYSTEM! Why does it work? It all works because of the Invisible Hand introduced by Adam Smith. That is the study of economics.

The Invisible Hand works really well as long as the governments involved do not interfere. As soon as a government, any government, in the entire chain decides that they will make it better, it automatically becomes worse and you may not even get your celery.

An illustration of this occurred during World War I. German submarines were sinking the ships bringing us the nitrates for ammunition, so we decided to build a plant to produce our own. Du Pont offered to build a factory to produce the needed nitrates. Many people in our government didn't want any private company to make any profits and they turned down Du Pont's offer to build the factory, and the government decided to do it themselves.

What was the result? Finally, after a significant period of time and failure of the government's plant, the government decided to have Du Pont do it. By the end of the war Du Pont built its factory for about $129 million and produced around 35 million pounds of cannon powder. The government's project, even with a significant head start, never produced any

11

at all! The full discussion of this can be found in the book *FDR's Folly* by Jim Powell on page 142.

That is just one illustration. For other illustrations, look at the entire history of the Soviet Union from the day they took over until they fell. You can also look at Cuba, which had a brisk economy until 1959 when the communists took over, and after that they couldn't support themselves. There is no limit to the illustrations of government's failure to perform the smallest economic task while the free economic marketplace performs it all the time without effort.

The result I am pointing out is that the Invisible Hand, using the economic marketplace, performs the extensive task of getting a stalk of celery to you all the way from Chile or anywhere else in the world at unbelievably low prices without noticeable effort. It is a marvel that it can do it. However, the minute any government gets involved it all falls apart.

There are two very important terms in economics that you should know: microeconomics and macroeconomics.

Microeconomics is simply the study of businesses and how supply and demand operates on a small scale. Macroeconomics is mostly the study of governments both international and national. That is just a simple way to keep track of these terms. There is a lot more to each of them, but those definitions are sufficient for this beginning book.

There are also two other terms that are not as important, but you will hear about them: elasticity and in-elasticity of demand and supply. They are simply a study of certain effects on supply and demand. Again, they can be very complicated if the professor wants them to be, but they are actually very easily understood.

Elastic just means that demand or supply can vary quite easily, and inelastic means supply and demand will not vary easily. For example, water in the desert is hard to get and therefore, is inelastic, and water in the jungle is everywhere, so it is elastic. That's not hard is it. That really is all there is to it, and we will not discuss elasticity and in-elasticity again in this book.

Another interesting concept discussed in economics classes is needs and wants. What is the difference between needs and wants? First consider needs. What do you need to keep yourself going? There are several basic items that you must have: air, water, food, shelter and clothing. Are there others? That depends on how and where you live. If you live on a farm your needs might also include barns and equipment to operate your farm. If you live in the suburb of a large city your needs might include a car and a phone. So, needs would be those items you require to live and those items you require to perform the tasks required for your survival.

But what are wants? This is a sticky subject. Some students say that they need a cell phone. I ask, what for? They respond by explaining that they need to call people. And I ask, why? The answer is usually for convenience. Is that really a need or just a want? Here is the problem. I have a cell phone that I use in emergencies, but it is never turned on, as I only use it when I need to call. I don't need to have everyone call me whenever they want to. I see people in the grocery store with a phone to their ear. Is that a need or a want? Let's consider cars. I must a have car for my business.

13

The question arises what kind of car? Do I need a top of the line Cadillac or would a Chevrolet or a Ford do just as well? Do I have a fancy car because I want it or is a fancy car required for my employment? Most of what we consider needs are really just high class wants. It's OK to have wants, just always realize that they are wants and not needs. Needs are for survival. Wants are for making life easier or fancier.

Role of Government

What is the role of the government? Simple, it is to keep the rest of us honest and make sure we deal fairly with each other. Anything more than this causes problems. People always look after themselves and their own interests. Sometimes individuals step on the toes of others and possible theft might occur.

So, the government's role is to set the stage for business and to keep it safe for everybody. That will also include keeping private property rights safe. Without government, some would steal what others produce. Without safety people wouldn't produce and the economy would grind to a halt. There must be an entity to protect citizens from theft along with protecting their interests, so the economy can flourish. If the government would just limit itself to keeping the peace, the rest would be taken care of by the economic marketplace.

Government must be supported in order to survive. A government produces nothing and, therefore, must collect money from its citizens. This is taxation. Originally, the federal government was very small and was supported with fees when goods were imported. Note Article I, Section 8, Paragraph 1:

"The Congress shall have Power To lay and collect Taxes, Duties, Imposts, and Excises, to pay the Debts and provide for the common Defense and general Welfare of the United States; but all Duties, Imposts, and Excises shall be uniform throughout the United States."

These import fees are actually paid by the citizens, as these fees will increase the price of the items that are imported. That provides a taxation system that is paid as people buy.

As time passed and government began to decide to take a larger role, more money had to be raised. Under the current unconstitutional tax system, it is possible for the government to tax away 100% of all profits and income. That would completely destroy the nation as there would be no savings or investment money available. It is also possible to return to the Constitution and delete the income tax completely. That would leave the money in the hands of the citizens and the businesses and encourage creativity.

The wealth of a nation is really determined by its manufacturing and production. Since taxation always lessens the production of a nation and its wealth, a government should keep taxation at the lowest level possible.

Returning to the Constitution would provide for the government's operations and leave as much money as possible in the hands of the people.

Today's unconstitutional taxation system allows the government to abuse the citizens by taxing at whatever level it wants and there have been instances where it has taxed at extremely high levels. Whenever taxes are high production slows down as money is lost to the productive portion of the economy. That is why, in our current taxing system, whenever taxes are lowered in such a way that businesses feel confident that the tax will remain at that level, prosperity increases.   And whenever taxes are raised business and prosperity declines.

That was the concept that President Reagan used when he reduced taxes and the economy prospered. That is the same concept that President Trump is now trying to do to improve the economy. Using government taxes to affect the economy either up or down is referred to as fiscal policy.

Fiscal policy is the policy of using taxation to either help the economy to prosper or to slow it down. This policy will either encourage growth or discourage growth in the economy. That is really the function of the Invisible Hand and it would work if the government would just get out of the way.

Monetary policy is the creation of money to stimulate growth. When we understand what the effect of the creation or destruction of money really means, we will understand that monetary policy will either cause inflation or recessions and therefore the pretended use of monetary policy is always bad.

When using fiscal policy, the lessening of taxes really does stimulate the growth of the economy because it creates more production without creating money. In fact, if there is more production without increasing the money supply, prices will decrease, and the citizens can have a greater variety of goods and services. In this way, the economy grows and becomes more prosperous. Fiscal policy works and monetary policy doesn't.

While increasing the money supply, monetary policy, has a temporary artificial effect of prosperity, it then begins to destroy the economy through inflation. When I was taught economics in the 1960s, we were taught that both fiscal and monetary policies were used to improve the economy in different ways. WHAT GARBAGE!! We were also taught that the federal deficit was needed to keep our country prospering. MORE GARBAGE!! That was and still is Keynesian Economics, which is the economics of deficit spending. And all of the students of economics during the 1950s, 1960s and 1970s, etc. were taught those principles from the books of Paul E. Samuelson. LOADS OF GARBAGE!! That is why so many economists of today believe in government spending to stimulate the economy. And they use items like economic stimulus packages, which fail every time, to do it.

At this point let's discuss the graduated income tax. The Sixteenth Amendment was and still is unconstitutional, but it still exists in the real world. In 1913 the graduated income tax amendment was passed, and it has been used ever since to provide money for our government. It has also been used to pay the interest on the national debt that was created by spending more than the government received.

Let's look at the basis of the graduated income tax. The concept is to collect more taxes from those who have more. The thinking is that a person who makes $20,000 annually will pay a greater percentage of his income for the basics of food and housing than someone who earns $1,000,000. Therefore, according to those who agree with this type of tax, the wealthy should pay a greater percentage of their income and this is called a progressive tax.

A tax that takes the same amount from rich or poor is considered a regressive tax. A sales tax is a type of a regressive tax. Notice the type of words used here. Progressive taxes take more from the wealthy and regressive taxes takes more from the middle income and lower income earners. Seems fair doesn't it. Well let's look more closely into this concept.

Where does business and industry get its money? The government doesn't produce anything, so business and industry are the backbone of our economic growth. Where does the money come from to accomplish this growth? It comes from savings and investments. If the middle and lower income earners spend more of their money on living and the wealthy spend less on living, who has more money left over to save or invest? The wealthy have that money.

If the government takes that money through so called progressive taxes, where will the money come from for the businesses? The maximum tax that the government can tax would be 100% of the extra income of the wealthy. That is the goal, by the way. Since they wouldn't have any extra money, where will the money for the businesses be found? Since there would be no money left over for business, there would be no business. Every dollar that the wealthy pays to the government is one less dollar available to create a job or an opportunity for you.

There is also another factor here. If you have $10,000,000 in your savings account, you know that if you spend it on a new business you could lose it. If you do not spend it, you will still have your $10,000,000. So, if there is little or no profit or return on investment because of high taxes, you will not spend it on the new business. The result of this is if the wealthy don't have extra money there will be no businesses to create the jobs for the middle and lower income earners. No extra money, no jobs it's as simple as that.

When government taxes the wealthy excessively, the wealthy do not spend their money on new businesses and the economy suffers. When the government taxes the wealthy less there will be more money available and more jobs. So, all that these people, who yell louder and louder that we should tax the rich, are doing is just cutting their own throats and their own opportunities.

That was how they got the progressive income tax passed in the first place. They promised the majority of the population, the middle and lower income earners, that the rich would pay for the government. Income taxes started at 3% only on the wealthy. Now look at history and see that the percentage even grew during the first year of its operation. Then, the income level decreased so that everyone paid taxes, not just the rich. After the tax amendment was passed the government immediately forgot what they had promised as it always does.

In conclusion, progressive taxes actually slow down the country's prosperity and regressive taxes actually better the economy. Progressive taxes take more money from the rich, which slows production, and regressive taxes take less money from the rich which increases production. The results are actually backwards from how they sound. That was done intentionally.

Now, let's move on to the next chapters where we will discuss the basic foundations of our freedoms: free markets and private property.

What Is an Economic System?

Here is a series of thoughtful concepts. Read each one and think about what they mean.

Every society has developed an economic system. How did that economic system happen? What would happen if it developed by itself, which means left alone with no government influence? Or what would happen if the government developed it?

Basically, there are two systems:

1. The market or the free system. This is the system that would develop if the government stayed completely out of it. It is the default system.

2. The command system. That is the type of system where the government takes control of the economic system and uses force to make sure that everything is done its way.

If government stops forcing the economy, it reverts automatically to the free system and operates for the benefit of the people. Why then is history so full of command systems?

The command system is deliberately used by an individual or group of individuals to achieve power, control and wealth.

Do not think of our system as capitalistic. It is a free market. All systems use capital as a basis. It is just who controls the capital that determines if it is free or controlled.

The major factors of the command system are:

> Government owns and controls almost all property
> Government decides what will be produced and
> how it will be done.

The major factors of the free or market system are:

> Property is privately owned
> The market makes the decisions

A major characteristic of the market system is private property, which is the foundation of a free economic system.

> What is freedom of enterprise?
> What is self-interest? Is it bad?
> What are the characteristics of free competition?
> Use of property how we want.
> Perform whatever labor we want without
> interference.
> Do we have this freedom now in America?

Here are five fundamental questions of how the market system responds in the economy.

1. What will be produced?
2. How will it be produced?
3. Who will get the goods and services?
4. How will the changes in the economy be handled?

5. How will progress be encouraged?

Let's look at each in order:

1. Items that are produced will yield a profit. Those that don't will disappear. Consumers buy what they want and need at the best price. (economic law)

2. Items will be produced in ways that have the lowest cost, and therefore will provide a profit by using the following:
The best location for distribution of that product,
The best technology,
The best use of resources including people.

3. The products will be distributed on the basis of what people want and their ability to pay.

4. The products and the systems of production can become obsolete. When this happens, the free market system will change the products and the production systems to meet the changes. This will occur because the consumers will not buy items that are more expensive, or not wanted, or do not serve their best interests. When a firm alters the item to better meet the needs of the people, changes will occur, and some products will disappear.

5. The society wants greater output, usually demonstrated by less cost per item, and that creates growth and progress. Also, the society wants better prices, usually demonstrated by a more efficient use of scarce resources.

Private Property

What does private property include? It is usually thought of as land. Is this the only thing that is private property? Think for a minute: if a building is built on the land, is it part of private property? A business must have machinery in the building to operate. Is that part of private property? What about the person who is employed by the business? Is his ability to labor a part of his private property?

You can see that property includes much more than just land. It can be described as any item that produces value. All activities that are part of production are the property of someone in the production process. Labor, resources, and capital are the basics of the economy and are always used in production. Therefore, they can all be thought of as private property.

Now think of the difference in the philosophy between the typical concepts of the Republican Party and the Democratic Party beginning with Franklin D. Roosevelt and continuing to today. Just listen to the campaign promises. Mostly, the Democrats promise everybody that the government will give them things. Where does the money come from to provide these things? It must come from someone else, as the government doesn't produce anything. Therefore, if the government provides a service, the workers of the economy provide the taxes to pay for it.

When everyone is working, they all pay taxes and they all receive the benefits. However, if there is a portion of the society that does not work, but still receives things from the government, the government must take the money from someone else to pay for it. Anytime you have money that is forcibly taken from you by your neighbors, that is theft, and your neighbor goes to jail for stealing. So, if the government forces you to pay taxes and then gives that money to your neighbors, the government has stolen that money from you and should also go to jail. In the United States today, the biggest crook in our society is the federal government.

Understanding the difference between a Republican (Free Market) and a Democrat (Socialist)

Fred Thompson and Hillary Clinton were walking down a street in Washington D.C., when they came upon a homeless person. The Republican, Fred Thompson, gave the homeless person his business card and told him to come to his office for a job. He then took $20 out of his pocket and gave it to the homeless person.

Hillary was very impressed, so when they came upon another homeless person, she decided to help. She walked over to the homeless person and gave him directions to the welfare office. She then reached into Fred Thompson's pocket and got out $20. She kept $15 for her administrative fees and gave the homeless person $5.

Now do you understand what socialism really is? Today we must be careful of attributing the Free Market to the Republicans. The difference between Republicans and Democrats used to be easy to see, but not anymore.

The differences are not so apparent today as they were 50 years ago, because the generations after mine have been largely taught that government is here to take care of us. The concept is the womb to the tomb. So, what is government doing with your private property?

Private property is much more important in the overall picture than just the land or the building that houses the business. Private property really embraces all parts of business life. If someone controls your life, he also controls your personal private property. Therefore, when a person says that without private property freedom cannot exist, he is really expressing the fact that we need to be able to control our lives in order for freedom to exist. Without private property, there is no freedom.

Now let's review real property and personal property. Real property usually refers to business property and equipment, or items that are used in production or to house the production. Personal property usually refers to items that are for personal use, household furniture, bedding, food etc.

So, can a resource be used as real property at one time and as personal property another time? For example, take for a car. When it is used for a vacation, it is personal property. When it used to deliver goods, it is real property. A building can be used as a residence, personal property, or as a rental, real property. Food can be eaten, personal property, or used as ingredients in a product to be sold, real property. Normally, food used as ingredients is considered inventory, and that is also a part of real property.

As you think of these items think in economic terms not tax terms. Taxes define some items as real property and others as inventory, and each is treated differently. We should always think of these items in the way that they are used, investment, real property, or consumption, personal property. The key is that they are all property in different uses, and for pure freedom to exist, all private property must be free of government control or restriction.

Free use of private property is the basis for free economic activity.

Where does property come from? It has existed from the beginning of time. Has there ever a time when there was no private property? Even though private property has existed throughout all history, there are those who feel that it must be abolished in the future for utopia to begin. In other words, they want to destroy freedom in order to have ultimate freedom. This is one of the ridiculous concepts presented by some who profess to be economists.

Think about this more completely. Will ownership of property really be destroyed under these systems? Or will the ownership of the property just transfer to someone else.

An example is the Soviet Union of the past. They said that everything belonged to the people and that everyone owned everything - the utopia, no private ownership. However, whoever controls an item owns the item. If I can direct how an item is to be used, I control that item and in essence own it, even if I say I do not. Now who owned the items in Russia? Who controlled them? The directors of the nation owned the property through their control of it.

Can owners of an item give themselves more of the item than they give anybody else? Of course, they can. Since they can do that and the leaders of many countries do give themselves more than they give to their people, they obviously own the items. However, that doesn't mean that they must give more to themselves; it just means they have the authority to make the decision of what everybody gets. Those who control the items own the items.

Where did they get those items? They took them from somebody else in order to give them to somebody else. It follows then that those who took the property and then redistributed it stole it and then claimed ownership of it so that they could give it to somebody else.

Consider private homes and land and buildings in the United States. As an example, when our private homes are paid for in full and the mortgage company or the bank has no more claim on them, who then owns them? Is it the person who has paid for them? That is what we are led to believe, but look again.

If you fail to pay income taxes, what does the government do? It fines you and forces you to pay by taking cash or value in some form or another and could put you in jail for not paying. If you fail to pay your property tax what does the government do? It takes your property and sells it!

When you owed the bank and you didn't pay them, they took your property and sold it, but that was proper as you hadn't paid for it. We knew that the bank still owned the property, but the government retains the rights to your property forever. If you have $200,000 or $500,000 or $1,000,000 in property and you don't pay a few thousand dollars of taxes, they can take it from you and sell it for a few

31

thousand dollars in taxes. Who then controls the property and who has the right to sell it? The government does and if they arbitrarily raise your taxes, you must pay the new taxes, or the government will take your property.

Therefore, in the United States who really owns all buildings and land? It's the government which controls the geography where the building exists, never the people who have paid for it with their hard-earned money. Remember the concept that whoever controls and can redistribute the property owns the property.

Remember a main purpose of government is to keep us honest in our dealings with our neighbors. Then the government has an obligation to ensure that our property is protected from theft. However, in our current society, and mainly from the Great Depression in the 1930s onwards the government has been the main source of theft of private property. It has not only stolen cash in the form of excessive taxes. It has also stolen value in the form of planned inflation. It has stolen opportunities in the form of zoning and business restrictions.

It has stolen profits in the form of restrictions on business in the form of licenses and regulations. It has stolen our formerly inexpensive medical system by causing tremendous increases on the cost of receiving medical care. It has stolen opportunities from the drug companies in the form of excessive regulation by the Food and Drug Administration. It has stolen cash in the form of increased taxes to give to the welfare system.

I have a list of over 1,000 federal government agencies that are unconstitutional and are stealing money from each of us. These agencies are then giving it to either themselves or to someone else as they administer these programs. In other words, our government has changed from a position of protecting us from theft to becoming the biggest thief in the country.

I mentioned the stealing of savings accounts and future retirements through inflation, but I would like to spend some more time on that subject. We do not actually realize how much theft the government performs in this area. These principles will be discussed in much more detail in other places, but for now know that as wilt any other commodity, creating more and more money causes money, like any other commodity, to lessen in value. As it lessens in value it can purchase less and less. The principle of losing value when too much is created also applies to local and international purchases.

When you hear that the price of oil has reached $100 a barrel or the price at the pumps is higher than it was last year. That probably really means that these is inflation or in other words more money has been created. This also applies to any other item that you purchase. When it has a higher price than it had last year, know that one of the main reason for that increase in price is because more money is chasing the same amount of production and goods. Since more money is chasing the same amount of goods, you must pay more to buy the same item. It is just as simple as that. If the government doubles the money in circulation either in actual dollars or in checking accounts or in government debt, then the prices of all items purchased with that money will also double. That is as sure as that the sun will come up tomorrow morning.

Current examples are the stimulus packages being "given" to someone. Stimulus packages is just a term that was invented to justify creating more money and giving it to a select group of people. These packages will increase the money supply through debt and therefore increase prices. If you could buy a TV today for $200 and there was an increase in the money supply of 10%, then in just a few months the price of that same TV will be $220 just as sure as it will snow in Alaska next winter. And if you save that $200 for one year instead of buying the TV you will receive about .25% interest for an annual return of $.50 and in one year the account will be worth about $180.50. The difference in buying power will be $39.50 and you will have to pay taxes on the $.50 earned. This is a small example of what is continually happening. Think of the compounding effect over 20 or 30 years.

This is what is happening to us in our economy. A chart of the money supply is available in appendix 2 to this book. The information was published by the Federal Reserve. And during the 5 years from 2001 to 2005, 3.720 trillion new dollars were created. That is 1/3 of the total government debt in 2005 and that was just over a 5-year period. That is the reason for the increase in prices. The reality is that if you save money to buy something, the government is making sure that you can never reach your goal. This is actually the worst theft of all.

Listen to the campaign promises of the presidential candidates of any election. They tell us how they are going to spend our money and there are no cheap programs. Put these campaign promises in their real language, and we see that they are really telling us how much more money they are going to steal from us for their pet projects. Our government is currently the biggest thief in our country. Organized crime is small potatoes compared to the United States Federal Government.

Capital Accumulation and Effect

Technological advances require additional capital. That encourages accumulation of capital. This is a term meaning the gathering of capital or money to begin a large business or enterprise. It is usually done by selling parts of the business through the sale of stocks. If the new technology is successful, profits will be distributed and the capital will eventually be returned through dividends or the increase in the value of the stocks. If the new technology is not successful, no profits and no return of capital results and the new technology will disappear.

Adam Smith introduced these concepts in *The Wealth of Nations* printed in 1776. He also introduced the concept of the Invisible Hand which explains how it all happens.

The term the Invisible Hand as introduced by Adam Smith was the force he felt guided all economic activities of an individual or society to the best outcome. The Invisible Hand is mostly composed of self-interest, greed and the competition in the marketplace as those are the natural thoughts and wants of mankind. Do not think of them as negatives but rather what life is all about. Self-interest is really just looking after your own best interests as long as it does not entail dishonesty and theft. Greed is the same thing. Competition is the natural way of things.

The keys of the best use of the resources of the market are:

Efficiency
Incentives
Freedom

Will the use of the resources be efficient? What are the incentives for the use of these resources in this way? Freedom to do what you want to with your resources.

Without all three of these, the free market collapses. Private property is the basis of each of these.

REMOVE PRIVATE PROPERTY AND LIBERTY
COLLAPSES!

Supply and Demand

When discussing economics, we must refer to Adam Smith who is considered the father of economics. As he wrote the book *The Wealth of Nations* he introduced the laws of economics, like supply and demand and the values of resources and labor. He referred to the controller of these economic laws as the Invisible Hand. No one person or any group of people can see the principles of economics work, but they are always there and functioning.

The law of supply and demand is the foundation of economics, and it cannot be controlled by society or government. The above law exists and cannot be changed by any government activity. Therefore, whenever more of the supply of an item is available than before, and all else remains the same, or all else being equal, the price will fall. Or the opposite, if demand for an item increases and supply remains the same, the price will rise.

In the booklet *Are We Good Enough for Liberty?* by Leonard Read there is a chapter titled I, Pencil, which is included as Appendix 1. This is an excellent demonstration of the Invisible Hand and shows how the law of supply and demand operates. The creation of a pencil is detailed along with the millions of people involved in its production. This illustration makes it readily apparent that even an item as common or insignificant as a pencil could never be created or planned by any government organization, or any other group no matter what the group's composition.

If any part in the creation or production of a pencil was lacking, the pencil would never materialize. Only a free society can possibility create a pencil. A government could not create it, because before its creation no one would know anything about it so they couldn't even start to plan for it. It couldn't be created since they wouldn't have the slightest idea what it is or that it is needed or wanted. Therefore, it would not exist in a planned society under government control.

An introductory discussion of supply and demand will discuss the following questions:

What is it?
How does it work?
What happens when a product becomes scarce or more plentiful?
Does it apply to items that are not purchased or sold?

To begin with, the supply of an item is the total of that item available from any source and the demand is a total of what everybody wants. We must remember that these concepts are all theoretical in nature and do not provide actual numbers, just directions. As you review the following graphs, take note that all of lines are straight. In real life they are not straight, but wiggly. That occurs because in real life there are many other important factors. Some of those additional factors are storage space, money supply, unemployment, taxes, culture, and environment to name just a few. For illustration purposes, we will keep the lines straight.

In some discussions about supply and demand, you will hear the terms elasticity and in-elasticity of supply and demand as mentioned earlier. These terms relate to how the above listed items effect supply and demand. For instance, if you lived in a desert, your demand for water will be different than if you lived in a jungle. Your need for water doesn't change, but the availability is vastly different; therefore, it will be more elastic.

In a desert, the demand for water will be very inelastic as people will do anything possible to get it including stealing from or murdering those who have it. In the jungle, the demand for water will be elastic, as there will always be more available almost without effort.

Our discussions will not cover elasticity of either supply or demand. The concepts are really not important as they are just variables and extreme situations to make the concept of supply and demand more difficult. That is what I mean by the phrase we teach practical economics for people not theories for professionals.

The following represents supply and demand as they occur in basic graphs. Look at graph #1 as shown on page 42. To begin with, notice how the lines are drawn. The line that begins in the upper left and goes to the lower right is called the demand curve, and the line that begins in the lower left and goes to the upper right is called the supply curve. The vertical line on the left indicates price of the item, and as you go higher on the line, the price rises. The horizontal line at the bottom indicates the supply of the item, and as you move to the right, more of the item is available. It is important to remember that as points or locations on a supply or demand curve change, it does not represent real price or supply changes. They only show the direction of the price or supply under particular conditions.

There are also two lines drawn from the intersection of the supply and demand curves, and these lines represent that the price and supply are in balance at that point. When either the demand or the supply changes, the graph changes and the balance point is lost, and the price will go up or down. The graph will also show that if the demand curve moves right or left, supply will move up or down until the balance reestablished. The next graphs will demonstrate the changes in supply and demand and the price changes at any given moment as different factors affect the supply curve and the demand curve.

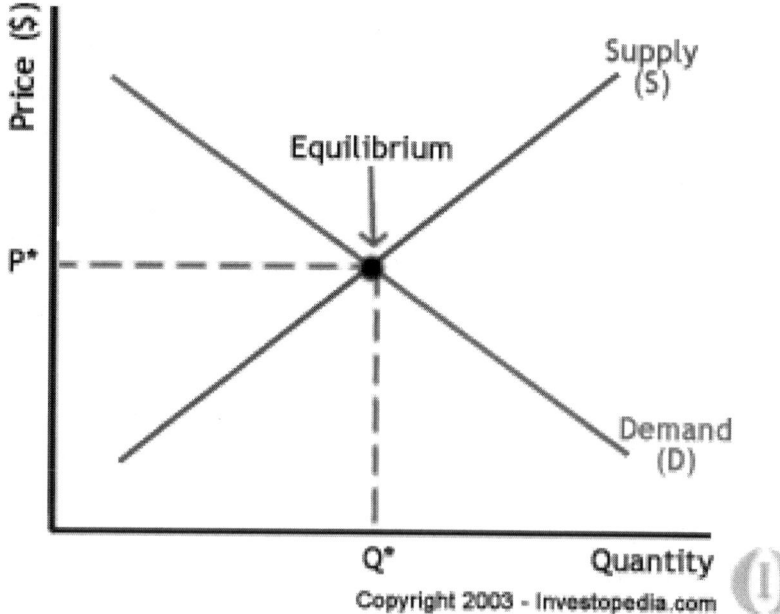

Graph #1

Here is how the graphs work. As shown in graph #2 when the supply curve S_t moves to the right to S_0, the supply increases, and the price goes down from P_t to P_0. There is more of the item available with the same demand, and the price falls.

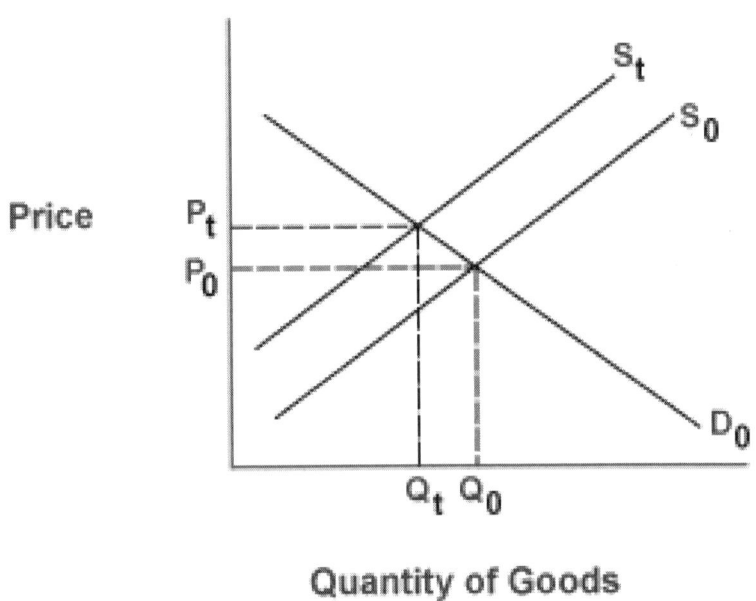

Graph #2

Graph #3 shows that if the supply of an item decreases, the supply curve moves in its entirety to the left, as shown in graph #3. As the supply decreases, Q_1 to Q_2, as long as the demand D stays the same, the price rises as shown by P_1 going to P_2.

Supply Shifts Left

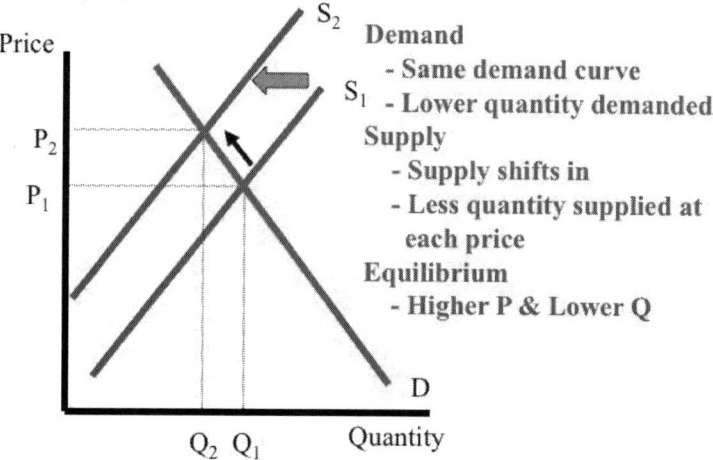

Graph #3

Now look at graph #4. When the demand of an item increases, the demand curve moves to the right, D to D¹, and the price will increase from 2 to 3.

Demand Increases

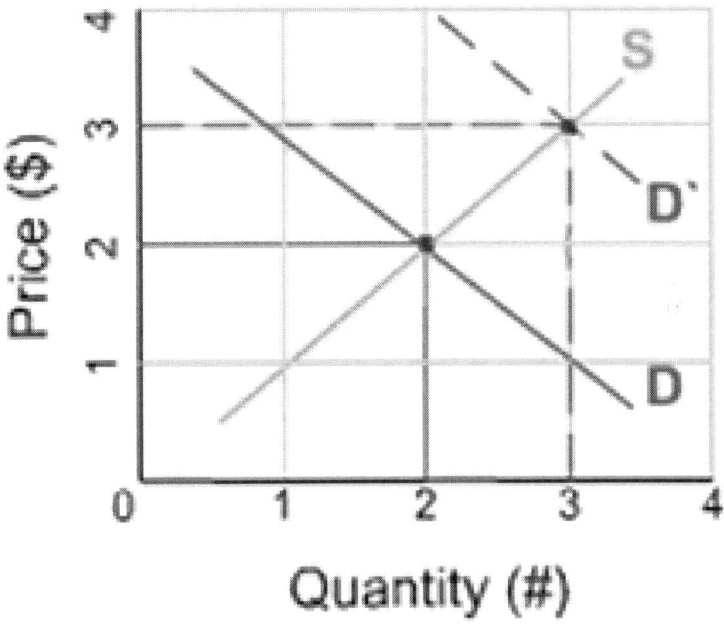

Graph #4

Then, as shown on graph #5, when the demand for an item decreases from D_1 to D_2, the demand curve moves to the left, and the price falls from P_1 to P_2.

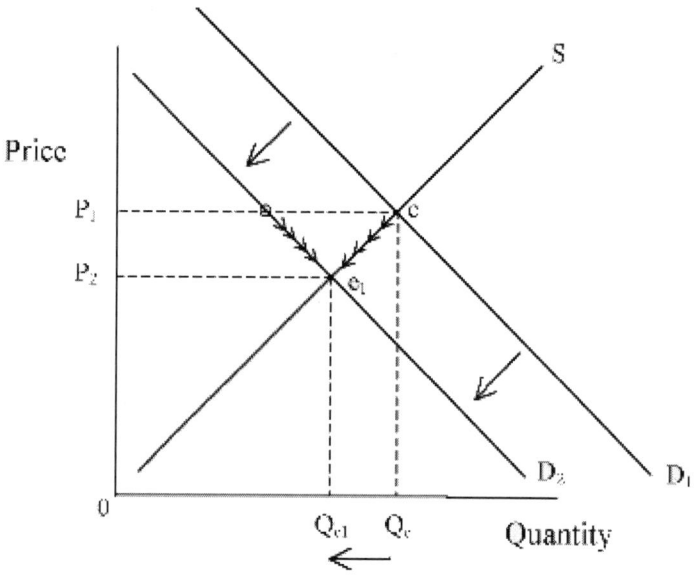

Graph #5

Another way to illustrate this point - as the whole supply curve moves to the right, more is available, and with the same demand, the intersection point will go down, indicating that the price is falling. As the whole supply curve moves to the left, indicating that there is less available, while the demand curve stays the same, the intersection point moves upward indicating that the price is rising.

Also, when the demand for an item increases, the demand curve moves to the right and if the supply remains the same

46

there will be a rise in price. And if the demand for an item decreases the demand curve moves to the left and if the supply remains the same the price decreases. These are the basic rules of these curves, and it is never more complicated than that.

Now let's use an illustration and see how it works in real life. Assume there was a company producing buggy whips, which was founded in 1825, and since their buggy whips were of the best quality, they did a really good business. Therefore, they produced all they could. Since there was a limit on how many they could produce during a one week period, the price was established at quite a high level. As the years passed, their business grew.

In 1890 as cars were introduced, their business began to decline as fewer people wanted buggy whips. Less demand, same supply equals lower prices. It looked like they were going to go out of business, and that would put quite a few people out of work.

So, they appealed to their representative in Congress to help them, and he introduced a bill that required every car sold to be equipped with a buggy whip. Now that buggy whip didn't serve any purpose, but it kept those people employed and the company making money, which was good for those few people. Of course, everyone else had to pay for a buggy whip they didn't want or need, but that didn't matter, the goal was met, and the company prospered, and those people voted for that representative again and again, and he stayed in office.

Ridiculous you say? Well that exact thing happened in the railroad business. When the diesel engines came along, the firemen lost their jobs, and soon after the brakemen also lost their jobs. Because of that, the caboose was no longer needed. So, Congress passed laws that the firemen and the brakemen had to be kept on. Because of that law, all trains had two employees that they did not need or want on every train, and the consumers paid the cost, exactly like the buggy whip company. Who really benefited in these cases, the majority of the people or the minority? A minority of a very few individuals were benefited, while the much greater population as a whole was damaged.

You say that was in the past and doesn't happen today. Well let's look something more recent - farming. Sometimes there is a drought and the crops die. So, what did the government do in the 1940s, 1950s, and the 1960s when the farmers suffered because of droughts? They passed laws to pay the farmer anyway. Sometimes there were excellent crop yields, because of improved farming techniques. Then, to keep the price up even though the supply increased, the government did two things. First, it bought up the surplus so that the increased demand would keep the price up. Second, it told farmers not to plant those crops, and that decreased production, which also kept the price up.

The government bought the extra crops that the farmers grew and paid the farmers for the crops that they didn't grow. Good, right? The farmers work hard, and they deserve to be helped, but who paid for these programs either in higher prices or higher taxes? The greater majority of the citizens of this country were damaged while the minority was helped.

I thought that I would participate in this bonanza, so I decided not to plant wheat in my backyard. I filed for the benefit from the government because I wasn't growing wheat. It didn't work and I was discriminated against. (That was just an example of the stupidity of this law. I really didn't do it.)

This is how the law of supply and demand works, and it cannot be altered by any government agency.

Here is another example that is closer to home. Almost every year there are severe hurricanes that plague the Southern States along the Gulf Coast. Whenever these hurricanes occur, homes in these communities are badly damaged and need immediate repair. A particular product is then urgently required, plywood. Plywood is a common item and is sold in locations throughout all of the country.

Where the hurricane occurs homes and businesses are destroyed or damaged. This includes the stores that sell plywood, but people will need large amounts of plywood to repair their homes and businesses. Since there is high demand for plywood and greatly reduced supply of undamaged plywood, the price goes up. Sheets that only cost $8 per sheet before the hurricane could go as high as $200 per sheet.

Because of high prices for plywood after a hurricane, the local government could pass what are called gouging laws to protect people against paying $200 for the plywood they need to make repairs. The gouging laws could set the price of plywood at $10 per sheet and penalized anyone who sells for more than that with severe fines. Everybody is protected and the price stays low. That is good, right?

49

Now look at what would have happened if the local government had just left the problem of the price per sheet to the law of supply and demand. What would have happened when the price was $200 a sheet? Plywood producers all over the country would immediately begin massive production because their costs would remain the same and their profits would skyrocket. They would get all the plywood possible to the area of the hurricane to take advantage of the higher price.

What would then happen to the price? Because of the greater supply, plywood would go back down to $8 or $9 a sheet automatically, and the people would have all the plywood they needed. It might even go lower if all of the shipments arrived at about the same time and created a surplus. That could lower prices to below the pre-hurricane levels, and that would be a good thing for the community.

What happened when the government got involved? There were unintended consequences. Since the government got involved, the price was controlled at the lower level, and it didn't encourage the production of plywood all over the country. Therefore, the citizens of the community had to get along with what was available in their area at the lower price. In effect, they had to do without a needed product. The price stayed the same so everyone could buy all they wanted of the nonexistent plywood at the normal price.

The government actually caused a shortage of a badly needed product. The area had to do without. The law of supply and demand would have automatically corrected these problems if the government had just stayed out of it. However, the temptation is too great, and politicians have to jump in for votes and feel good remedies. KEEPING GOVERNMENT OUT IS THE VERY BEST POLICY EVERY TIME!

Another government intervention occurred during the period of extreme inflation during the 1970s. Richard Nixon was President and the government froze wages and prices for 90 days. The result was constant requests for waivers and a buildup of pressure for the higher wages and prices that the market demanded. Then, when the 90 days were over, everything immediately jumped up to what it would have been without the freeze. Nothing was solved because the Invisible Hand that Adam Smith spoke of in *The Wealth of Nations* just kept on working regardless of what the government was doing. The laws of economics do not abide by government decrees; they just go merrily on their way.

We discussed this of concept supply and demand in detail because it is the most important and least understood of all the laws of economics. Every time I teach an economics class I stress, the need for the government to stay out of the business world, and I always have arguments from the students that the government must have a hand in the economy of the society to protect the people. We have become a people depending on the government every time a difficulty lies in our path. What happened to self-reliance? Supply and demand will also play a significant role during the next discussion of money.

Money

In an introductory discussion of money, the following questions arise:

Where did money come from?
Why did money develop?
Who creates money?
How much money should there be?
Does the amount of money determine the economic
    life of the society?
If the economy is stable, not changing its size or the
    standard of living, what will happen:
    1. If more money is created?
    2. If money is destroyed?

The discussion must then include banking:
    When and how did modern banking begin and why?
    What is fractional reserve banking?
    Why was fractional reserve banking developed?
    What is the purpose of central banking?
    Who benefits from central banking?

What is compound interest?
        What are the pitfalls or benefits of compound
interest?

Money originated back in the mists of time. In the beginning, however long ago that was, people exchanged items between themselves through a system of bartering. However, there was a significant difficulty. How did you get some wheat while bartering with a cow? Something had to be used to make up the differences, and money was introduced. In the beginning, selected objects were used, such as salt, sugar, special stones, and other items. Later gold and silver were fashioned into coins, which became the common form of money. Eventually paper was introduced.

It didn't matter what was used, gold or silver or paper, as long as everyone recognized and accepted it. Then how much of the item was available became the important factor. Remember supply and demand.

Today in the United States who creates the money we use? In Article I, Section 8, paragraph 5 of the Constitution it says that the Congress should create it and regulate its value. In actuality, our money is created by a private corporation called the Federal Reserve. The government asks for the money it wants and the Federal reserve creates it. So, the government doesn't create it.

Who regulates the value? That must be answered by explaining how the value of money is regulated. As mentioned before money is a commodity and the value of a commodity is established by how much of it there is. If there is a lot of money the value decreases and prices go up. It takes more of it to buy something, and we call that inflation. The more money there is the faster prices rise. If there is a shortage of money the value increases and prices go down. It must be better for the economy when prices go down, right? However, when prices go down companies can't make enough money to keep their production up, so they lay people off. When they lay people off, the people have less money so they buy less and more people get laid off. This is called a recession or a depression. So, if there is an excess of money there is inflation and if there is a shortage of money a recession or a depression occurs. Both inflation and recessions are equally bad. So, it is necessary to keep the amount of money stable so people will have confidence in the economy.

The story is told of an island cut off from all other islands. They used white shells as their money, and there were 1,000 shells available in the society. The people who grew the coconut trees wanted two shells for each coconut people wanted to buy.

One day while out swimming, two brothers came across a large bed of white shells. When they counted them, there were 1,000 shells. They collected them without telling anybody and hid them. Then, whenever they wanted something, they just used some their newly found white shells. As they used their shells the supply of money increased while demand stayed the same. There were no more products than before, just more shells. As time passed, eventually they used all of their white shells, and an interesting thing automatically occurred. The price of coconuts became four shells instead of two, and everything else also doubled in price.

Here is another illustration about how creating or finding more money changes the true value of the money? Let's select a product, say shovels. This is a basic item with little variation. First, set the number of shovels at 1,000 with a price of $25.00 each. Therefore, we could say that $25,000 is tied up in shovels. The amount of $25,000 will remain the same in the first illustration of our model. There is only $25,000 available for shovels. Now if the number of shovels expands to 2,000, and since there is only a total of $25,000 available for shovels, how much will each shovel be worth? $12.50. More goods chasing the same amount of money. The economic jargon is more goods, 2,000 shovels, chasing the same amount of money, $25,000.

Now let's reverse the whole thing. Instead of holding the money at $25,000, let's hold the supply of shovels at 1,000. If more money is created by the government and the amount for shovels grows to $50,000, how much will each shovel cost? $50. That means that the money has lost 100% of its value, as it now costs twice as much for the same item. The value of the money is lost as the amount of money increases. All of the prices in the entire economy will be affected in the same manner. In our example, everything will double in price. This happens because of more money chasing the same amount of goods.

There is yet another story to illustrate what happens to the economy when money is printed. Assume you are at an auction, and the dealer presents an item of value that you really want. However, this auction will only accept cash, no checks, loans, or credit cards. While biding for this item, you quickly discover that several others in the audience also want it. You check your pocket, and you only have $266.26. The biding starts low but is fierce. Some others must have more money in their pockets than you do, and you're frantic to have the item. Then you notice a sly gentleman in the back of the room giving people something whenever they ask for it. You go back and discover he is handing out $100 bills, so you get some. Now you are confident that you will have enough. However, the bidding continues to rise, and you run out of money again. You look frantically around the room, and the man is still there. You go and get more money from him, but the bidding still goes up and up. Everyone seems to want that item, so the price is approaching $1,000. Now here is the question. Is the value of that item growing as bids increase? Of course not. The bidding is going up because there is more money available in the room.

That is how inflation works. As the supply of money increases, the prices of the items in the country go up because the people have more money to spend. It has nothing to do with value; it has everything to do with the amount of money available. Refer to Appendix 5 DVD # 9.

Let's consider another thought. Some professors in economics classes and some books written to teach economics maintain that inflation is caused by rising prices. They ignore the changes in the supply of money. That is similar to saying that wet streets cause rain. Wet streets are a by-product of rain not the cause, just as rising prices are a by-product of the increase of the supply of money not the cause.

These examples are just stories with no actual numbers attached, but they illustrate the point that inflation is caused by the printing of money. The economic law is that there is more money chasing the same amount of goods or services. It is the Invisible Hand at work. Whenever a community or society has a limited amount of money and a limited amount of goods and services, any change in the amount of either of them will always cause a change in the prices. This is a very important rule.

Whenever a government prints or issues more money, and the products available do not rise in the same proportion, prices will rise. Conversely, if more products are produced and the money supply and demand remain constant, prices will fall. There is an economic formula, MV=PT, that illustrates this concept. This formula was taught in all basic economics classes prior to the beginning of the 1960s. During the latter part of the 1960s and since then, this formula has not been taught. The concept that took its place was one that says - inflation is caused by rising prices. Refer to Appendix 5 DVD # 10.

That is also similar to teaching that the stripes on a horse turn the horse into a zebra. Since the animal was born without stripes it was called a horse, but as time went by it developed strips. As the stripes occurred, the hide changed and the horse became a zebra. Now that is ridiculous, just as the wet street illustration is ridiculous!

There was terrible inflation during the 1970s. This was a fierce inflationary period in our country. In fact, it was worse than many realize. The inflation rate rose to around 18% or so, and the interest rate also rose to around 18% or so. That meant that each year prices rose at about a rate of 18% while the interest was also increasing by around 18%. If you add these two numbers (which you should never do as it is mathematically incorrect) the total effect of the increased money supply in the 1970s could have been around 36% a year, and wages didn't change hardly at all.

Back to the economic formula MV=PT:
M = the money supply;
V = the velocity of the money as it travels through the economy;
T = the number of transactions during a set period of time; and

P = price.

M or the supply of money is a precise number. V and T are computed through the mathematics of econometrics and are also exact numbers. P is a direction and does not represent a number. During the calculation of price, a number is derived but the number only indicates the direction since the last calculation of the price, not an actual amount.

If you move the numbers around, according to the laws of algebra, you can do this.

Divide both sides of the formula by T and the result would be: $MV/T = P$.

Or it could be written as M multiplied by V divided by T equals P or $M* V/T = P$.

Now if you arbitrarily set both V and T equal to 1 they cancel each other out and the formula becomes is M=P.

This is very important, as it clearly shows that as the money supply goes up or down so will prices.

Why do you think that the formula is no longer taught? Because some with power do not want people to realize that the precise cause of increasing prices is the increasing of the money supply. They want everyone to think that inflation is caused by rising prices to hide what is really happening. Look at Appendix 2 - the Money Supply of the United States from 1931 to 2006. These numbers are from the Federal Reserve's actual reports. Take some time to look at how the money supply increased during the 1970s, and think about the inflation and the interest rates during that period.

The next question to ask is who created that money and why? They are the same people who own the Federal Reserve, which is helping to create the huge yearly deficits in the United States. Those deficits keep the national debt constantly growing. They are the same people who are profiting by that huge national debt. Who are these people who are profiting from our huge national debt? They are part of I call the International Banking Establishment! They own the Federal Reserve and therefore, spread the profit among themselves.

What is the International Banking Establishment? It is a small group of very wealthy European bankers that want more wealth. They also want power and control over everyone else. The current group was organized in 1776, and they called themselves the Illuminati. One of their major goals has always been world domination. Two of the tools they are using are education and economics to gain that control. This group of people and their activities are included in my series of books titled *Liberty: Will it Survive the 21st Century?*

Back to the profits of the national debt. What does the International Banking Establishment do with this immense profit? They bring it back to the United States to buy the politicians who are running our country. Where did you think all of the money comes from that is used to control our elections? Some of it is the money that we pay as interest on the national debt. That money comes from our hard work and then it comes back to us through control of our elections. If the members of Congress do not vote for what the International Banking Establishment wants them to, they cut off their funds and someone else gets elected, that will do the bidding of that sinister organization. That's why the Congressmen are always doing things that are against our country. The International Banking Establishment wants the New World Order, and to get that accomplished the Constitution must be abolished along with our system of government. To do this those of the International Banking Establishment use our own money to destroy us.

This explanation still did not answer the basic question of why these people are doing this. A first thought that we must remember is that people always want more money and more power no matter how much they already have. Some individuals actually have an addiction to money and power and can never get enough. With this in mind, they have also set themselves up to acquire all of the interest from the banking profits.

On May 1, 1933, during President Roosevelt's administration, it became illegal for Americans to own gold, and our currency went off the domestic gold standard. Later Gold was also pegged at $35 per ounce for international transactions worldwide. All international trading was conducted in U.S. dollars per the Bretton Woods Agreement. The Federal Reserve was prohibited from creating more money than was allowed, based on the value of the gold we had stockpiled in Fort Knox which was the gold repository for the United States.

As long as the world expected gold to be $35 an ounce for every dollar, there was a control on how much money could be created. The powers behind the scene had to do something about that! Another part of this dilemma was the fact that we were, and still are, the reserve currency of the world. A reserve currency is currency from another country used as the foundation of their money. Other countries use our dollar to back their currency. If we changed the value of the dollar, it would be felt all over the world.

What did the International Banking Establishment do about that $35 per ounce problem? During the late 1960s some European nations, primarily France, decided that they wanted the gold that they had on deposit in the vaults of United States at Fort Knox. They began requesting that their gold be shipped to them, and gold was shipped from the United States to Europe. Every time a shipment was made, our gold supply decreased. We did not have to make these shipments, but we did. As the supply of gold in Fort Knox decreased, our country got closer to the limit set by the $35 per ounce requirement. There were all sorts of speeches made in Congress about this problem, but we still voluntarily kept sending the gold. The problem became more and more critical, but Nixon and the Congress just kept authorizing the shipments. Finally, we got to the point that something had to be done.

The first step was to create a two-tier value for gold. For all international trade transactions, we would continue to keep gold at $35 per ounce, but the world market price of gold would be determined by the market. Immediately the value of gold on the open market went clear up to $39 per ounce and then to $45. Now unintended consequences began occurring. Countries began to get gold from us at $35, and then they sold it on the open market for whatever they could get for it. This was a major problem that could not be controlled by the United States. Finally, the two-tier system was abolished, and we went completely off the gold standard. There was now no limit to the amount of dollars that the Federal Reserve could create, and they got busy.

Where did the money that the Federal Reserve created go? It went to European banks and companies and it became a part of the M3 money supply.

Banking

Let's choose the year 1533 and visit that renown township of Gliberhaven (fictitious) in central Europe. and review the close friendship of the prosperous merchant Henry, and Levi the goldsmith. Henry had extra money that he had difficulty keeping secure, and Levi had a strongbox which Henry knew had extra space available. So, Henry approached Levi and asked if he could rent some space in his strongbox. Levi agreed. They set a nominal fee for the storage, and modern banking was born.

This arrangement between these two friends worked very well. Whenever Henry needed additional money, he went to Levi and requested it from the storage in the strongbox. Levi always obliged him and took Henry's money from the strongbox and gave it to him. On the other hand, when Henry had extra money, he took it to Levi, and Levi put it in the strongbox.

Since money was going in and out at irregular intervals, Levi devised a system of receipts so that there was a record of how much money Henry had in the strongbox at any one time. This was very satisfactory to Henry, as he was able to keep better track of his money.

As this system worked so well between him and Henry, Levi offered some space to George, Bill, and Gary. They each agreed to the arrangement, so they also set up provisions for their money. The receipts then carried the name of the individual to better keep all of the deposits separate.

Now Levi was making additional money by renting out the extra space in his strongbox, so he decided to offer the opportunity to additional friends and bought a bigger strongbox. Levi was receiving a substantial income by renting out space in his larger strongbox.

In addition. since Levi was a goldsmith and usually better off than others in the area, individuals from the township of Gliberhaven and the surrounding area regularly approached him for loans. Levi was often able to assist them, and they paid him a fee based on how much they needed and how long they planned to keep the money. Today we call that fee, interest.

Now Levi had an interesting thought. He realized that the individuals with deposits didn't come very often to ask for money from the strongbox. In fact, most of the money was never touched it just sat there. Based on this experience, he decided that since the money was just sitting there doing nothing, he could make some additional money if he were to loan out some of that money also. He would insure that he didn't loan out too much so that there would always be money available if one of his depositors requested it. Thus, fractional reserve banking was born.

As time passed, he kept records of how much of the deposited money was out at one time, how well the borrowers paid, and the size of the idle deposits. He also began to tell others that he had space to rent, and as time passed, he began to lower the fees to attract more depositors. He realized that he made more money on deposits and loans than he did as a goldsmith, and since he always followed his most profitable opportunities, he began to concentrate on getting more and more deposits.

He was now very sophisticated about how much money he absolutely had to have on hand to meet the demands of his depositors, so he began to loan out more and more of the deposits. This was quite a profitable scheme. The danger was that he always had to have money on hand to meet the depositors demands. Sometimes it was so close, he had to dip into his own funds to ensure that he could pay the money out when it was requested. Once he even had to postpone a depositor for a few days while he got the money accumulated that the depositor was requesting. This was a real problem, so he began to keep a little bit more for safety's sake. The amount that he decided he had to keep on hand was 10%, and that was almost always safe.

This little story about Henry and Levi of the township of Gliberhaven, is how banking initially got started and why fractional reserve banking became so popular. Others saw the opportunity and set about to copy Levi. Some of them were not so honest, and they were often short of money. Sometimes the depositors grew afraid that their money would not be there when they wanted it, so they withdrew their money and put it with someone else in whom they had more confidence. Today, we call those times when people withdraw all their money, runs on the bank, and today's bank runs are caused by exactly the same reasons as those bank runs in Gliberhaven were.

As time passed, larger and larger banks were organized, and it became necessary to have the banks band together to assist each other in bad times. When banks began to band together, they usually formed a central bank for their organization. This was a real boon because the central bank could set rules that all the other banks had to follow.

Next the central banks discovered that when the government asked to borrow money, all they had to do was create it. They got the interest whether they actually gave the government money from their vaults or just created it with accounting entries. Corruption set in, and the central banks never even bothered to keep any money. They just printed it when it was requested, and everybody was happy. That is everybody but the citizens of the country, because as the central bank printed more and more money, inflation started and the prices of everything began to rise.

The government of Germany really got behind the printing of money beginning in 1921. The penalties of the Treaty of Versailles to end World War I were such a burden on Germany that it was impossible to make the required payments. So, the government just printed the money needed to meet those obligations, and the hyperinflation in Germany of the 1920s began. This action was a separate case though. It was not a central bank that printed that money; it was the government of Germany itself: good for the government, bad for the people. However, it's very hard to stop hyperinflation once it gets going. It required over five years to get it under control, and it destroyed the economy of Germany.

Who owns banks? They are corporations just like any other corporation. They sell stock to raise the initial capital to start up just like any other corporation. So, a bank is owned by some individuals. What about a central bank? At first it was usually owned by the banks in the organization. So, by extension a central bank was owned by the owners of the banks in the organization. Later the central banks began to authorize the banks and eventually set it up so that the central bank not only controlled the banks but essentially owned them. Then who got the profits of the central banks if there was any? The owners of course.

What is important to know about the Federal Reserve of the United States? Who owns it? In 1913, the Congress enacted the law that allowed the Federal Reserve of the United States to be established. Then early in 1914 the organizers issued and sold stock for ownership of the bank. Who bought the stock? The large banks of the United States did. All on the up and up. Right? Well, who owns the large banks of the United States? The largest banks of Europe own our largest banks. Who owns those banks? The European financiers own them.

So, what did I just write? The major financiers of the European financial world own the rights to print the money of the United States. That power gives them the ability to control the issue and value of the money and also to control all of economic parts of our country. They decide how much money to print, what the interest rates will be, what kind of growth we will have, what our unemployment rates will be. They decide EVERYTHING THAT DEALS WITH FINANCE, EVEN THE RULES TO OPEN A BANK ACCOUNT. They require you to provide your fingerprint to open an account. That fingerprint is then digitized and sent to Europe to your master file. Refer to appendix 5 DVD # 10.

We have given our lives to the European financiers, and we don't even realize we did it! Will that knowledge will help you sleep tonight? You'll never find anyone in any banking institution who will admit this, but it is happening. The European financiers are the bosses who run our banks.

Let's take a look at the national debt. The debt is created as the government borrows money from the central bank of the United States, the Federal Reserve. That debt creates profit for the Federal Reserve, and those profits also go to the European financiers. Currently we send approximately $500 billion or more to Europe every year just in interest on the national debt. Then every year our Congress just makes this debt larger, and we send more of our hard-earned money other there. The people in Washington D.C. are really looking out for us, aren't they!

Remember the discussion on fractional reserve banking? Who determines how much money the banks must keep in reserve? The Federal Reserve does and currently that is around 10%. Therefore, when the International Banking Establishment decides that they want to keep more of your hard-earned cash, they only have to increase the amount that the banks must keep of the deposits.

Let's analyze how this is done. In the previous paragraph we learned that the banks are normally required to keep 10% of the deposits. What if that amount were increased to say 11%? Then instead of having to keep $1,000 out of every $10,000 they would have to keep $1,100. That small change reverses the creation of money to the destruction of money.

That is the kind of event that happened in 1932. The banks were required to keep more of the money, and therefore could make fewer loans. In addition, they had to call in loans that had been previously issued. This destruction of money causes the economy to begin to slow down and collapse. The size of the collapse depends on how large the additional deposit requirement is and how long that requirement is kept in place. We are in the hands of the Federal Reserve Bank, and it can do whatever it wants.

We call these events of the destruction of the money supply recessions and depressions, and they are controlled by the International Banking Establishment through the Federal Reserve. For example, we had a depression in 1836 that occurred because the bankers were angry that the charter of the Second Bank of the United States wasn't renewed. The bankers could cause another depression in our country whenever they want to and for no reason at all except that they wanted to. We are at their mercy, and they have no mercy.

This was a brief demonstration of how the current banking system controls our economy. Our labor is stolen from us through both inflation and direct theft with recessions and depressions. These ups and downs are called business cycles, and they are caused by the Federal Reserve.

A constant drain of value is stolen from our economy through this system, which is just smoke and mirrors, and was created by the enactment of the Federal Reserve Act in 1913. However, that was not the first time it had been done. These concepts have been going on ever since the fractional reserve banking system was created. It was a part of the First Bank of the United States in 1791, and that bank was created under the influence of Alexander Hamilton.

The Second Bank of the United States was chartered in 1816. Then in the late 1820s Andrew Jackson saw what was happening with the economy of the country and prevented the renewal of the charter in 1836. The European bankers saw their profits dry up, so they created recessions and depressions in the United States regularly throughout the 1800s. Then Paul Warburg was sent here in 1906 to get another central bank started. This time they avoided the problem of a charter that would expire and set up the Federal Reserve without an ending date. We have been saddled with it ever since, and whenever anyone tries to stop it or reveal it, that person's career is destroyed. The money tree must not be disturbed, and the American people must pay the bill.

Now, are your sure that you can sleep at night?

The next part of this deception has to do with keeping the people comfortable. If the people get nervous about their money, as they did in the early 1930s, there must be something to calm their nerves. So, the government created the Federal Deposit Insurance Corporation or the FDIC. Because of the monetary problems that the Federal Reserve created in 1932, the FDIC was enacted and signed by President Roosevelt on June 16, 1933. The FDIC was intended as an insurance program for Americans. Is it of any value? Refer to Appendix 5 DVD # 4

It was established to provide confidence to the people that their money was safe. I remember in the 1950s thinking that since the FDIC would protect my money up to $100,000 per bank, I should plan to spread the money out over several banks to keep it safe. We all understand insurance to be a protection against loss, and, therefore, if our bank balances are protected by insurance, we feel more secure. However, does the FDIC really protect our money?

First, we must better understand insurance. Insurance is a medium of protection for a series of random events. If an event can be planned or anticipated at a particular time or during a particular time frame, it is not insurable because it is not random. Home fires and death are random events and do not occur to everyone at the same time and are therefore, insurable. If an event happens to everyone at the same time or it is not random, then it is not insurable. The so-called FDIC insurance does not cover against a random event, nor would that event happen to only a part of the insured. Therefore, it is not insurable. When bank failures begin, the problem very quickly effects all banks in the community and the affected area grows very fast.

Now is it viable? To understand this, we need to look at the resources available to protect our money. Approximately 1% of the necessary funds for the protection of our accounts is held by the FDIC. Therefore, if there were a run on the banks, which is the reason for the insurance, could it satisfy the requirements? It could not without printing or creating more money.

Here is a possible scenario. The banks begin to fail nationwide, first one then another. As the first banks begin to fail, the FDIC would step in and provide the funds necessary to protect the customers. These first failures would exhaust the funds available. Then as other banks began to fail, the FDIC would have to appeal to the Federal Reserve for more money to bolster up its viability. Since the funds to back up

73

the commitment were not sufficient, money would have to be actually printed or created to meet the needs of the situation.

If the FDIC were to have to cover all bank accounts, enough money would have to be printed or created to save every account. Hopefully, after the system was able to show that it actually had saved some banks, the population would calm down, and the bank run would stop, and the customers would return their money to the banks, and business would continue as usual. However, if that did not occur and the scenario continued to the bitter end, the Federal Reserve would have to print up to double the money in circulation, which would then create significant inflationary pressure of up to double. Since it is not really insurance and the reserves are so low, it is really another kind of fake currency. The cure would be as bad as the disease, as the public would lose its money anyway through massive inflation.

The FDIC is a tool to keep us happy, but in reality, in the long run, it has no value for its customers or the population.

Why do banks fail in the first place? It is because the depositors fear the loss of their money. So, in any market at any time, if the depositors took their money out of a bank, it would fail! Here is an interesting example. In Hong Kong, a line near a bank caused a run on the bank, and it failed along with other banks before the panic calmed downed. The first bank was stable and operating normally with proper reserves, but the depositors caused its death and the loss of their own money!

Remember classic movie, It's A Wonderful Life? In that movie, the Bailey Savings and Loan was saved because

George Bailey convinced the depositors to take out loans instead of canceling their accounts. Their money was still in the bank, and I'm sure they paid back the loans. The Bailey Savings and Loan survived. He kept the depositors from closing the bank and losing their money. So, the following two statements are accurate:

Only the depositor's actions can bankrupt
an honest bank!

If the depositors leave their money alone,
an honest bank will never fail!

The result is that the FDIC is just a band-aid. It actually has no function except to deceive us into thinking that because of the FDIC our funds are safe. The government has deceived us into believing that that organization keeps our money safe. We are at the mercy of the Federal Reserve and it has no mercy!

Compound Interest

We must not neglect a discussion on compound interest. What is compound interest? Here is a definition from Wikipedia:

Wikipedia
January 2016

"Compound interest is interest added to the principal of a deposit or loan on a daily basis so that the added interest also earns interest from then on. This addition of interest to the principal is called compounding

"Compound interest may be contrasted with simple interest, where interest is not added to the principal (there is no compounding). Compound interest is standard in finance. Simple interest is used infrequently (although certain financial products may contain elements of simple interest).

When a chart is created to show the difference between simple interest and compound interest, it shows that there is very little difference at the beginning. With a deposit of $10,000 in the first year the difference is only $51.56 more than the interest received from simple interest. But the effect is phenomenal when followed for many years.

Now consider what the significance would be if you took out a loan from a financial institution instead of making a deposit. Now the benefit is for them and against you. In this type of arrangement, you are charged interest every day on the full amount outstanding on the loan. Every day the loan grows by the interest on however much you still owe. If you are late paying the monthly amount, you will be assessed a fee in addition to the interest.

Most loans from banks are set up in such a way that if you are early in the month with your payment you will still pay the full interest for the entire month, including the full interest for the days you paid early. Some loans will not let you prepay without a penalty, which means that even if you pay the loan completely, you will still pay some interest on money you have already paid back. When you borrow money, be very careful to read and understand the payback provisions, because after you sign the document you cannot change it! Compound interest can be a huge burden unless of course, you are the individual that benefits and gets the money.

Now that you are more aware of what borrowing can cost you, can you see why paying cash is always the best way? If you already have this interest burden you are paying, get out from under it as fast as possible. Make a plan and then stick to it. Refer to Appendix 5 DVD # 2

By the way, there is money the financial institution earns on your deposits in addition to the interest you pay. The banks create money out of thin air when they make loans. They have no risk as they don't really provide you with any money. Since there was no money paid out when they make a loan, they can keep all of the money you pay on the loan. They call it capital investment and they turn around and loan out that money also! Banking and especially central banking is a real gold mine, without even considering the control created over the citizens of the country. Since these banks are all private institutions, all of these profits go to the individuals who own them, and those people are eventually the European financiers.

And as if it couldn't get any worse, the central bank created by Congress in 1913 was ILLEGAL. It was and still is UNCONSTITUTIONAL. Read the Constitution Article I, Section 8, Paragraph 5 and you will see that Congress is given the responsibility of coining money and establishing the value of it. Congress passed the law that created the central bank in violation of their oath of office to uphold the Constitution. All of these individuals raised their left arm and placed their right hand on the Bible and swore an oath to uphold the Constitution, just as is done in court. In court you can be jailed for violating that oath. Who are these people representing?

Deficit Spending

What is deficit spending?   Basically, it is a government spending more than it collects.   For a complete picture, we need to review one of the most influential men in economics during the 1930's: John Maynard Keynes.

In the 1930s, Keynes caused a revolution in economic thinking, overturning the older ideas that said free markets would automatically provide full employment.   Keynes argued that aggregate, or total demand would determine the overall level of economic activity, and inadequate aggregate demand could lead to high unemployment.

According to Keynesian economics, state intervention was **absolutely necessary** to control the economy and all economic activity.   He advocated the use of government measures to lessen the adverse effects of recessions and depressions.   That was one of the original goals of the Federal Reserve, and they have failed at it completely.

Did you notice the term, "inadequate aggregate demand?" That is the foundation of all of Keynesian economics, and it is just a concept of smoke and mirrors and lies.   The foundation is incorrect, and the whole concept fails.   The term means that there is a shortage of demand in the economy, and the government must correct it by spending more.   What garbage!

It works like this: since there is a shortage of demand, the government must spend more to create more demand.   How does the government do that?   It does it by spending more than it collects in taxes.   Where does that money come from?

It comes from borrowing. Who does the government turn to in order to borrow money? It turns to the people within the economic system.

Therefore, it boils down to the following: The government needs money to operate. It taxes the people to get that money. If it spends more than it collects, it borrows that money from the same people it taxes. Therefore, the people have less to spend by the exact amount that is borrowed.

The government then spends that money and claims it has created more demand. However, in fact, the people have less money which means there is less demand by the people. Then the government spends the money it borrowed. It spends exactly the same amount that it borrowed.

An illustration would look like this. The people have $10,000 and the government has $5,000 for a total of $15,000. The government wants to spend $8,000. The government then borrows $3,000 from the people and leaves the people with $7,000. The government now has the original $5,000 plus $3,000 for deficit spending for a total of $8,000. The people have $7,000 left. The total of both the people and the government is still $15,000. There is no gain. The same amount was spent, just from a different source, government instead of people. The people spend less and the government spends more by the same amount.

Therefore, there is no such thing as government fixing inadequate aggregate demand. The term inadequate aggregate demand was made up to create a problem that didn't exist in the first place.

This idea has been foisted on the American people since the 1930s when it was made up by Keynes. The national debt was created by this idea, and now the debt is over $20 trillion and cannot be paid. The cure will be terrible. Therefore, this concept set up a situation that will cause the complete failure and total destruction of our economy.

All economists, since the 1930s, have had this concept drilled into their heads by every professor of economics that they had. I thought it was valid until the 1970s when I saw that the economies of West Germany and Japan were prospering without deficit spending. Therefore, I looked more closely at what was actually going on and discovered the facts shown in the above illustration. That principle simply states X out from one part of an economic society, and the same amount of X in from another source within the same society equals zero change.

Then, in mathematics if you ever divide by zero, the solution is always wrong. However, a formula can be devised, so that somewhere in the formula of symbols and calculations, division by zero is snuck in. Then the result you get is impossible. That must be the type of analysis that Keynes used in his calculations to hide the truth.

Keynes' book on this subject is among the most complicated economics books available, with very complicated formulas, and somewhere in these, formulas he must have effectively divided by zero. Since this conclusion was reached by one of the most revered economists of our time, everyone accepted the conclusion without doubting how he got there. Thus, all of Keynesian Economics is probably based on the concept of division by zero and was forced upon us by a man who was a Fabian Socialist.

The Fabians are the individuals that brought the *Communist Manifesto* into the modern era. They brought that book, which was in obscurity, to the front and began teaching and encouraging it. They are responsible for the Russian Revolution. As a group they formed the catalyst that caused the socialist ideas to take hold all over Europe. There are around 8,000 members worldwide but they are so well hidden that I cannot find an adequate membership list. John M. Keynes was one of them and look at the damage he has done to the principles of economics.

Most prominent economists, have accepted Keynes' theories and they have been completely misguided because of the author's reputation. We must note that his reputation was created by the same people who own the Federal Reserve. His system provided billions of dollars of profit to the Federal Reserve and thus their owners every year. Do you notice the conflict of interest? No wonder they agreed with it. It made money for them by the truck loads. I suspect in private Keynes laughed at us and wondered why we were so stupid.

There is another part of the deficit spending discussions that is another lie. This lie is that our economy must be based on debt and that if we stopped our deficit spending policies our economy would collapse.

This is the reasoning: Government spends money for projects throughout the nation. As it spends money it creates jobs. The government has so many projects and it must borrow money to finance them all. If the government stopped borrowing money, some of the projects would not be developed and jobs would be lost.

Also, if the government paid off some of the debt, there would be even less money available for the projects and even more jobs would be lost and this would be a total disaster. Therefore, we must continue to borrow to finance these government jobs and never pay off the debt. Our economy depends on debt to survive. This doesn't even pass the smell test!

Let's look closely at the basics of the argument mentioned above. It's jobs. All strong and vibrant economies rely on jobs, not debt. The key for the growth of an economy is jobs and production. Our economy, and all others, relies on jobs and production for economic growth, not debt. Since jobs are the key, the government should stop destroying jobs by excessive taxes and regulations.

The concept of debt to stimulate and develop the economy is a major lie put forth by the International Banking Establishment and the Fabian Socialist Society to control our lives. Their goal is to get us to depend more and more on the government so that the government can get into the little details of our lives. Total slavery of the entire nation through false economic principles is the intent.

Here is a story taught in many economics classes to demonstrate how production helps the economy. There was once a grocer in a village. One day some kids were playing around his store and broke his window. The grocer then had to purchase a new window, and that provided work for the people who sold the glass, and the people that got the sand for the new glass. The people who bought the sand from the miners and the people who transported it to the company that made the glass also did more business.

The people who made the glass produced more and those who made the items to hold the glass in place also benefited. The people who transported the glass to the grocer and those who manufactured the trucks that carried the sand and the glass also produced more.

The people who developed the gasoline that powered the truck, the people who transported the gasoline to the store that sold the gasoline, and the people who sold the gasoline also gained. Those who made the containers that held the gasoline and the people who installed the glass produced more and so on. The professor then would say, in all his wisdom, "Look, do you see how much was produced to replace the glass and all of the benefits that the new window would contribute to the community?"

After this story is told, an astute student would then raise his hand and ask: "What would the grocer have spent the money on if he did not have to replace a previously good window pane? Wouldn't that have done as much for the community, and wouldn't that have been a more positive direction?" That student was usually ridiculed, and if he persisted in these comments, would probably have failed the class, or at least received a poorer grade. I know that because I knew students who asked those types of questions. I was enthralled by the professor and understood all of his reasons. I hadn't yet had any life experiences.

This concept of more and more production is used as a basis for some government policies and has a major fallacy. If this illustration of the broken glass was actually correct and would be the best thing for the community, wouldn't it be better to constantly destroy the buildings, roads and everything else. If we destroyed everything look at all of the production that would be created and how much better the community would be. What stupidity! However, there are many economists that agree with this and maintain that wars are beneficial because of all of the reconstruction that they cause.

Here is an illustration that some economists use to demonstrate that the national debt is no problem at all. It is also based on a faulty foundation. The example involves ten businessmen who decided to build a golf course. They formed a corporation, which then borrowed $10,000 from each of them. The $100,000 was used to build the course, and they could play golf for free whenever they wanted. They also allowed others to play for a fee, and thus they were earning some money back. The important part was that since they each owned part of the company, and that company owed each of them $10,000, there was really no debt. The company could be debt free by just deleting the debt. So, the debt doesn't matter.

However, if you look closely at the situation we and our government are really in, it doesn't fit the story at all. This is because the Federal Reserve, the company making the loans, was not and never was owned by the people of the United States. That was just a farce they foisted on the public by calling it the Federal Reserve. It has nothing to do with the federal government. It was and still is a private corporation owned by the European financiers.

Therefore, we never borrowed the money from ourselves in the first place. Then these financiers want their interest and the possibility that the money be paid back. The purpose of the "loans" from the Federal Reserve was to get the American people deeply in debt. There never was any money to loan; they just quietly created it to provide the loan. The result is that the national debt as of the end of 2017 is over $20,000,000,000,000. This is money that never really existed in the first place, and that number is so big we really can't comprehend it.

Another part of the national debt will now surface. Some of the national debt is owned by foreign people and nations. This was real money that they loaned us, and they really do want their money paid back. Here is another economic fact: United States dollars can only be spent in the United States. Every foreigner who accepts United States dollars must spend those dollars in the United States to get back the value they gave up.

And here is another problem of deficit spending: the trade deficit. There isn't really any trade deficit. Every item that is purchased must be paid for. A trade deficit simply means that we purchased more goods from other countries than we bought from other countries.   Therefore, dollars went overseas to pay for those goods and that money balanced the transaction.

Since dollars can only be spent in the United States, how are those dollars redeemed? Foreigners are using them to buy land and businesses in the United States. Are you beginning to see some of the problem that we are in? What will you think when every piece of land and every business in the United States is owned by a foreign individual or country?

This is what the International Banking Establishment has been striving for. Have you heard of the New World Order or the World Economy? Both of these are being developed by our constant deficit spending, or in other words by the overspending by Congress and the Executive Departments. We are spending ourselves out of existence.

In 2013, many in our government wanted to raise the national debt limit, and when the House of Representatives wouldn't go along, the Executive Department began closing the country to force them to do so. The government threatened to stop the checks to the social security recipients and to stop the welfare checks. There was such a clamor that the debt ceiling was raised so we could all get our money.

No one even considered cutting spending and stopping all the unconstitutional government operations. Just doing that would have balanced the budget with money to spare. In 2006 there were over 1,000 government departments that were all unconstitutional, and we still pay for them each and every day. Deficit spending has brought all of that about, and deficit spending provides the government with more and more power over the people every day.

In April of 2017, we again faced the problem of the debt ceiling. By the way, this is a farce perpetrated on the American people. The debt ceiling will always be raised, so why is it there in the first place? Government always wants more money and will always get it if it can be borrowed.

We have been in a quagmire for a full century, and no one has had the common sense to get us out of it. Around 50% of the population of the United States receives money from the government, and that is a major part of the deficit. We are spending ourselves into bankruptcy. Educators and parents never teach children self-reliance anymore. We are teaching them how to get money from the government. And since we are stealing from our future the price will eventually be paid.

Minimum Wage

Basically, a minimum wage is government imposed it's a form of socialism. At first glance and without much thought, minimum wages seem like a very good thing. When minimum wages started in the United States many considered it necessary. Wages seemed to be very low. Even now there are people, maybe even some adults, who are not earning what is considered a living wage. That's when the "take care of everybody, and keep them safe" folks enter the picture. The first instances of this "fix" was small and didn't seem to amount to very much, but later the concept took on a life of its own.

The actual economic factors work like this. Each time the minimum wage is increased, the individuals in the lowest wage group receive an increase. What is not considered, except by those who are paying attention, is that the others working in the same company see that the difference in their pay and the pay of those that work for them is diminishing and this is demeaning to them. Therefore, they seek and get a raise comparable to the increase of the minimum wage that the others received. The result is that all wages in the entire country are affected. Therefore, every time the minimum wage is raised, all other wages are also raised.

Then, since wages are one of the biggest costs in production, the prices of the products must be raised to ensure that the profits remain in an acceptable relationship to what they were before the minimum wage increase.

In many cases technology, which was not even a consideration before, is put in place to reduce the number of employees and thus keep wages under control. Other wage cost saving measures are also put into place by just eliminating the lowest level jobs or what is commonly considered the entry level jobs.

The people of the older generations remember when there were ushers at the movie theaters, gas station attendants who looked after your needs when you stopped to get gas, and many other entry level employment jobs performed by teens just entering the work force. Those jobs and opportunities have disappeared, and teens no longer have opportunities that help shape their lives.

The largest effect is on the retired. Many of them have fixed incomes, and the increase in costs reduces how much they can buy. They have to scrimp and do without to the detriment of their life styles and health as they age.

In actuality, there is no benefit to minimum wages. For sure, the wages are increased for those at the lower employment levels, and it did help those people for a few months. However, within six or so months the prices caught up with their new wages, and they were right back where they were before the raise. Another effect not usually considered was that the businesses found themselves unable to reward better employees with pay raises. The employer was forced to tell those employees that the government had already given them and everyone else the raise they would have been entitled to. Since there was little reward for better work ethics, they lost the incentive to do better, and the attitude became so what, I'll get the raise soon enough without any extra effort.

Minimum wages destroy the economy while pretending to assist. This is always the result when government tries to fix problems that the free market is already handling.

Economics is not usually taught at the high school level. As it seems to be a difficult and complicated subject, students avoid it even when they are in college whenever possible. Because of this lack of education, few learn what is happening and they are led to the slaughter by government officials who claim to be helping them. However, these so-called helps are just to get their votes. The politicians don't care at all whether or not new policies do any good. As long as the voters think they do good, and they get reelected, so what?

During 2016 a new program for giving away tax payer money surfaced. It is called Universal Basic Income (UBI). The idea began in Oakland, California and then was considered in Hawaii in 2017. Now, Stockton, California is expected to become the first US city to launch an experiment in universal basic income, a system of wealth distribution in which people receive a set amount of money just for being alive.

Stockton Mayor Michael Tubbs said that by August 2018 he hopes to enroll an undisclosed number of Stockton's 315,000 residents in the program. Tubbs said the experiment, which is set to hand out $500 a month, or $6,000 a year, would ideally last for a period of three years.

Where does the money come from to pay for it? The first source of the money would be from the citizens of Stockton. After that the funding could come from the state of California and finally from the federal government. But the real source of the funding will be from working Californians and American citizens. If taxes are not enough to pay everybody, then the money will be raised by borrowing. In either case the working individuals will have the money stolen from them to give to others.

What will be the outcome of this type of program? People will become more dependent on the government for their livelihood. More will go on the government dole, which means more will receive, and need, free stuff from the government. Children will be taught that they cannot live without government help and a further generation of welfare recipients will be developed. Some working individuals will discover that they can receive more money by idleness than they earn by working and will quit working. The final result will be a further weakening of the greatness of America,

The concept of welfare, as it has come to be defined, has been one of the greatest threats to our country and its citizens. It has bred an entire population of people that cannot take care of themselves. When they were children they properly depended on their parents while they were developing. Then they graduated to a new set of parents, the government, and they stopped developing and became stagnant with no personal ambition. We would do well to eliminate the entire welfare system, not add to it.

Free Trade

The first part of a discussion of free trade is to define what it means. Economically it means trade between countries with no tariffs or import fees or restrictions, etc. Simply put that means that a company from Germany can take its goods and move them into the United States free of any charges for entry into the United States.

Article I, Section 8, Paragraph 1 of The Constitution says:

> "The Congress shall have Power To lay and collect Taxes, Duties, Imposts, and Excises, to pay the Debts and provide for the common Defense and general Welfare of the United States; but all Duties, Imposts, and Excises shall be uniform throughout the United States;

There it is, Congress should collect duties, imposts, and excises to pay for the operations of the government. These items are normally referred to import taxes or taxes on items imported into the United States. That was how our government received money to pay for itself during our first 135 years as a country, and it worked.

Is there more behind tariffs than just raising funds? Yes. tariffs will protect the manufacturers and industries of the country from foreign imbalances. What do I mean by foreign imbalances? These are the differences in the cost of living between countries. In addition, foreign imbalances occur when the governments of some countries support their industries financially. Therefore, governments should protect manufacturing and employment through the use of tariffs.

The main reason for tariffs is that some countries are very poor and have significantly lower economic standards of living than others and, therefore have lower labor costs. To protect a country from countries with lower labor costs, the governments of the countries with higher labor costs support the companies in their country with tariffs. That way those companies can still produce their goods and services and be profitable.

Another reason for tariffs is to protect war manufacturing industries. Some countries want their manufacturing base to be protected so that if there is a war they will have the means within their borders to produce war materials. Tariffs and duties can be used to protect the war manufacturing industries of the country.

Tariffs have been used ever since international trading began, and they have served various purposes. There have even been tariff wars. Tariff wars happen when one country raises its tariffs and others retaliate. One of the main functions of embassy consulates is to help sell goods of their home country in the foreign country where they are located. Trading is a very important part of the economy of all of the countries of the world. For example, where do we get most of our tropical fruit?

Early in his administration, President Trump started to implement tariffs. Some noticed that tariffs would raise prices on goods from overseas, so they called it a border tax and began an assault against it. They were right, tariffs do raise prices on imported goods. However, those against tariffs never mentioned that the reason for tariffs was to protect domestic industries, and that means protecting American jobs. The lack of tariffs destroyed full industries here in the United States which, which led to the destruction of millions of jobs. Tariffs, properly used, will recreate those jobs. So, those fighting tariffs are also fighting against job creation policies. Do we really want fewer jobs, which also results in less economic growth? Refer to Appendix 5 DVD # 1.

Now that we have learned a little about the problems of trade, let's get back to free trade. How is the International Banking Establishment using free trade to further their objectives? Entire industries have been destroyed in our country by our government's policies on importing goods from other countries. How did this happen?

In economics, the Law of Comparative Advantage explains the idea. In the 1700s, our country was very similar to the world in general. Things were beginning to improve, but so far it was just a start. As time passed the Constitution and our newly created form of government provided a free society which allowed everyone a free opportunity to profit from their ideas. We took advantage of these conditions started on a path of tremendous growth.

During the 1800s, as we were somewhat isolated by the Atlantic and Pacific oceans, and our government didn't attempt to control our businesses, we began a period of economic opportunity never before experienced. We grew at a rapid pace, beginning to outstrip all of the rest of the world by leaps and bounds. Finally, in the 1900s, we arrived at a point where we were without question the wealthiest country in the world. We lived like kings in comparison to most of the world. The only part of the world that was anywhere near our standard of living was the Northwestern part of Europe.

Now why was this the case? It occurred mostly because of the freedoms granted by our Constitution, but that was not all. Everyone did that which they could do best, and that raised the whole of the society. This is what The Law of Comparative Advantage is about.

This is how it works. Let's take two people who live next door to you - an attorney and his secretary. The time of the attorney might be valued at $150 per hour, and the time of the secretary might be valued at $20 per hour. The secretary works 8 hours a day for the attorney and earns $160. The attorney works for his clients for 8 hours a day and earns $1,200. The total value to the community is $1,360 per day.

Now, let's change the situation; they separate and go to work for themselves. The attorney does his own secretarial work, and the secretary attempts to do the attorney's work. Because the attorney cannot do an adequate job at the secretary's tasks, it takes him longer to do them, and he can only do 3 hours a day of attorney's work while doing 5 hours per day of secretarial work. Meanwhile, the secretary can't do any of the complicated work of the attorney so she works 8 hours doing menial attorney tasks but still only earns $20 an hour. Her total is still $160 (maybe).

At this point, the attorney's total income is only $550 per day, $450 of attorney work and $100 of secretarial work. The total to the community is now only $710 a day. This is a loss to the community of $650 per day or nearly 50% of the original total.

Now I'm going to ask you the two dumbest questions you've ever heard. If there were an attorney just down the street who only charged $25 per hour and you knew he was just as qualified as the one next door, what would you do? What if the attorney knew of a qualified secretary just down the street that he could hire for $3 per hour, what would he do? Sounds stupid, doesn't it? But that is exactly the effect of free trade when you live in the wealthiest country. Unemployment occurs because the most expensive workers will always be unemployed! And no government can change it! Laws can be passed, but those laws cannot change the economic laws.

Let's apply that idea to the states of our country. We have a vast climate difference. throughout the USA. The states in the South can raise citrus fruit for next to nothing in comparison with the Northern states. The Northern states must erect greenhouses to raise citrus fruit, and the cost in the winter is prohibitive.

The only way the Northern states can survive is to get the state government to establish tariffs on all citrus fruit coming into the state. That would raise the prices of citrus to levels high enough to allow the greenhouse operation to be successful. Everybody is damaged, the people in the South because they lost some of the market and the people in the North because of the high prices that the population would have to pay for citrus fruit.

The major reason why the United States is so successful in comparison to the rest of the world is that we have no trade barriers between our states, and everybody within the same government does that which is best for them: The Law of Comparative Advantage shows why companies and people to do that which is best for them in their climate and location. And the Constitution provides a control on the states that prevents them from erecting tariffs between states. In Article 1, Section 10, Paragraph 2 we read:

"No State shall, without the Consent of the Congress, lay any Imposts or Duties on Imports or Exports, except what may be absolutely necessary for executing its inspection laws;

Based on the economic success in our country, many economists contend that if we were to have worldwide free trade and access to all the markets of the world like it is in the United States, every nation's standard of living would raise to ours. However, we must look at the population and conditions on each side of the event before we can make that assumption. Appendix 3 is a nearly complete listing of the countries of the world and their standards of living as of December 2014. We are third from the highest. As shown, only 5,634 million people live above our standard of living. Everyone else lives below our standard of living.

In other words, something we purchased for $20 in our society, with a standard of living of $41,557, would be purchased for much less in over 99% of the world. For example, Timor-Leste, in South-East Asia, has a standard of living of $400 per year and the same item that was produced in this country for $20 could be produced in Timor-Leste for maybe 19 pennies. Or put in another way, someone working in our society who is paid $20 per hour would earn 19 pennies an hour in Timor-Leste.

The number of the people in the world who live below our standard of living is 6,580,000,000. Our population is small in comparison; and since the disparity between our standards of living is so great, the only outcome would be to lower our standard of living to levels we would not like. That is what worldwide free trade would do to us after a few years. It would not be all at once, but we would experience it very quickly.

One more item could be addressed in this discussion. What would happen if one of the companies of the United States moved to Timor-Leste? First, the firm would begin to produce products employing the people of Timor-Leste. What do you think they should be paid? If they paid 19 cents per hour, some of the do-gooders in our country would yell and scream, protesting that the firm was taking advantage of the economy of Timor-Leste to make more money. These do-gooders would demand that the company pay a living wage. What is a living wage in Timor-Leste? In the United States, it would $10.00 or more an hour. What would happen if that was the pay offered by the firm to the people in Timor-Leste?

Everyone in Timor-Leste would quit the jobs they had and flock to the new company. That would mean that many of the services in the country would not have the employees needed to get their work done. Then, as these people were paid, they would spend the money like they were kings, and they would be kings in relation to the everybody else in their society.

Money would flood into their economy through the wages from that company.

Do you remember what we discussed earlier about more money chasing the same amount of goods and services? Prices would rise. Would the wages from the rest of the companies in Timor-Leste rise also? No, they would stay the same. Can those people survive if that imbalance continued for very long? No.

If the company from the United States paid too much, it would essentially destroy the economy of Timor-Leste. So, in spite of the hollering by the do-gooders, the best policy is to pay the normal standard of wages for that country and make more money. Just having the facility in the society will enhance the total community, and that is a good thing. However, paying wages beyond the normal for the area would be disastrous.

Now what would happen in our society if all of the goods produced in Timor-Leste, and countries similar to Timor-Leste, came to the United States market based on their labor costs? Everyone would buy the products from Timor-Leste, and our workers in the same industries would lose their jobs because the companies could not stay in business, and extreme unemployment would result. What if this happened in most of the nation? Our standard of living would decrease.

In Pat Buchanan's book *The Great Betrayal*, he shows the results of free trade coming into the United States. He discusses the textile industry at great length. He shows how the policy of free trade completely destroyed our textile industry and devastated many cities and towns as the demand for their products dried up and left most of the people unemployed. That is a good thing for the other country, but what about the people of our own country? Many employees are at the later stages of their lives. They must move to new cities, learn new trades, and compete with the younger generation or starve.

Remember, if a company can produce in an environment that is more profitable, it is in their best interests to do so. In fact, if they do not, then there is a distinct possibility that they will go out of business. So, the real question is, why did our government establish conditions that would encourage our industries to move their locations to foreign countries?

Another illustration is the plight of the grain farmers. In the 1950s, we were a major exporter of grain to the world. Today, according to the U.S. Grain Council, in 2012 the United States grew nearly 10.8 billion bushels and roughly 7% of the production was exported. Only 7%, what a fiasco.

The problem is worse for the wheat producers. My brother-in-law farms over 200 acres of winter wheat and sells it for less than $7.00 per bushel. Three or four cups of that wheat can make several loaves of bread that could sell in our stores for much more than $7.00.

Why does he receive such a low price for his grain? It is because he competes with the world market, where the farmers make just a few dollars a day. He sells his product at the world price and lives here in the U.S. where he must pay U.S. prices. This equation cannot be sustained. When we allow free trade with another country, that usually means that our industries will dwindle and die.

In the modern era the Republicans under Ronald Reagan and George H. W. Bush began to abandon the protectionist ideology, and came out in favor of the polices of minimal barriers to global trade. Free trade with Canada came about as a result of the Canada-U.S. Free Trade Agreement of 1987, which led in 1994 to the North American Free Trade Agreement (NAFTA). It was based on Reagan's plan to enlarge the scope of the market for American firms to include Canada and Mexico. President Bill Clinton, with strong Republican support, pushed NAFTA through Congress over the vehement objection of labor unions.

Then in 2000, Clinton worked with Republicans to give China the most favored nation trading status, meaning low to no tariffs, and our markets began to be flooded by products from China. People who were pro NAFTA deceived us with promises of an optimistic vision of the future. They maintained that there would be new prosperity under NAFTA. This new prosperity would be based on intellectual skills and managerial know-how more than on routine hand labor. They promised that free trade meant lower prices for consumers and greater markets for our manufacturers. The result was actually lower prices for mostly inferior goods and the loss of most of our manufacturing base and the jobs that went with it. Then down went our standard of living as wages decreased.

Then many other free trade programs between the United States and other foreign countries caused disastrous results for our economy. The United States currently has free trade agreements in force with 20 countries. These are:

Australia   Israel

Bahrain	Jordan
Canada	South Korea
Chile	Mexico
Colombia	Morocco
Costa Rica	Nicaragua
Dominican Republic	Oman
El Salvador	Panama
Guatemala	Peru
Honduras	Singapore

In addition, there were many politicians who wanted another free trade agreement called the Trans Pacific Partnership Trade Agreement (TPP). This is an ambitious, 21st century trade agreement in which the United States negotiated with 11 other countries throughout the Asia-Pacific region including Australia, Brunei Darussalam, Canada, Chile, Japan, Malaysia, Mexico, New Zealand, Peru, Singapore, and Vietnam.

If this free trade agreement had been finalized it would have been the death of the rest of the production and manufacturing here in America. Why are our own representatives trying so hard to destroy our country?

The Law of Creation of Value

I have discovered an additional economic law that, as far as I know, has not been previously observed nor discussed. It answers the reason for the greater affluence of the United States in relation to the rest of the world during the same time period.

Here are the conditions that create the increased value. First, there must be a significantly isolated population. That means that the population is relatively isolated from the rest of the population. That is usually accomplished by large geographical boundaries which can be within the same country. This isolated population will increase as new people move into the area. Secondly, everyone is working for the betterment of all, based on their own ambition. That means that each will freely work at the job which is best for his skills.

As more and better products are produced in this community by the efforts of each person, the standard of living will increase. This is because everyone will be industriously working for his own benefit. As the standard of living increases in this isolated community, prices and wages will increase, regardless of what is happening in the areas around them. This is not inflationary growth but real growth because of new products and product improvement of existing items and overall better quality. The result of this is that the community as a whole becomes more and more affluent and all values increase.

The new values are created by increases in price while keeping the total supply of money constant. The change in value occurs in a small community even though the community is a part of a larger population or nation. The larger economic system is controlled by the government of the nation which controls the value of the money by increasing or decreasing the money supply. As these changes occur the small somewhat isolated community becomes more prosperous as they work together to improve their economic conditions regardless of what the larger system does. Values will grow faster in the isolated community than in the larger total of the actual nation.

The community can be as large as a country, like the United States during the 1800s, or as small as a significantly isolated group within a country.

Wealth is then created through the process of allowing goods and services to grow in value within the designated group. Early in its history, the United States grew in affluence while significantly isolated from the rest of the world. We became more and more wealthy as the goods and services in our country became more and more valuable. This must not be confused with inflation, as inflation is caused by an increase in the money supply with no offsetting increase in the value of the goods and services. When the money supply is kept relatively constant and the value of the goods and services within the isolated population increases, an increase in wealth occurs. As time passes and the value of goods and services continues to increase, more and more wealth is created. Refer to Appendix 5 DVD # 9.

The United States was significantly isolated from the rest of the world during the 1800s, and slowly the prices of goods and services increased through the diligence of the population, while the money supply remained relatively constant. The money supply is the key to the prosperity. Prices always change but the value changes because the money supply remains the constant.

In the United States we experienced challenges when the money supply increased or decreased. However, the value of goods and services almost always trended upward, creating a more prosperous society in comparison with the other nations of the world.

As the wealth of this isolated community grew, based on the increasing value of the products within it, the group would have extra money to bring in other products from the general population around them. Conversely, if the value of the products remained the same and did not increase in value, there would be no extra wealth created, and the people of the group would experience the same standard of living as those around them.

Based on the outcomes of the cooperative effort of the group, others would join the group, enticed by the results and encouraged to participate in its increasing growth and success. The more people in the group, the more solid it becomes. As time passed, the standard of living of those in the smaller group would surpass that of the rest of the population. This group would form a nucleus within the larger population which would eventually raise the economic level of the entire population.

In summary, The Law of Creation of Value requires a cooperative effort by a small group of individuals whose intent is to help one another achieve the levels of economic prosperity they desire.

National Debt

I have created a table, appendix 4, of the national debt of the United States as of January 1st of every year since 1791. Since the best result is always to decrease the debt, I marked those years with a decrease with an "xx". Here are some interesting facts:

- Since 1956, or for 62, years the national debt has never been reduced.

- Starting with 1981 every year's debt increase was $100 billion or greater except for the year 1999 when it was only $17 billion.

- Starting with 2007, there were 7 years with an increase of more than $1 trillion with one year at $1.8 trillion. That $1.8 trillion year increased the annual interest for that year and every following year by $4.5 billion.

Both main political parties have been a part of these debt increases, which means that neither of them have had our best interests in mind at all.

An increase in the national debt is always bad even if the increase is less than it was the prior year. It is interesting that many politicians claim there is a decrease in the national debt when in that fact that decrease is just something less than they borrowed in the previous year, but the total debt still increased overall. Then remember there has never been a decrease since 1956 and the increases since 1981, except for the year 1999, have never been less than $100,000,000,000!!! Every year those bandits in Washington D.C. steal more and more from our country's future with their outrageous spending of our money, and as a consequence they make our country poorer.

The table in appendix 4 includes a total of 228 years and indicates the below interesting statistics.

The national debt has been reduced only 80 times or only 34.9% throughout our country's history of 229 years.

From 1913 to 2018, the debt reduced 17 times which is only 16.2% of the time. I selected 1913 because that is the year that the Seventeenth Amendment moved the election of the Senators directly to the people rather than their being appointed by the States. This removed one of the most important safeguards against the federal government's excessive spending. We deviated from the Constitution, and therefore allowed the federal government to spend without control. Beginning in 1913, all financial checks and balances were removed.

After 1929, we became a welfare and socialistic culture and needed more money in the federal budget to support these costs. The easiest way to get money is to borrow it. The Federal Reserve was established in 1913, and one of its major goals was to loan money to the federal government. Therefore, in the period from 1929 to 2017, debt was reduced only 5 times, which is only 5.6% of the time.

This lack of government fiscal responsibility was accompanied by a decrease of self-reliance after Franklin D. Roosevelt's social programs were enacted. Prior to 1929, the national debt had been reduced 75 times, or 53.6% of the time as compared to the measly 5 times after Roosevelt. However, a more meaningful percentage would be to note that 93.75% of the reductions of the national debt occurred before Roosevelt with only 6.25% occurring after his presidency.

This demonstrates a complete lack of any fiscal responsibility. This pattern was then followed by the States. The States now are also more than a trillion dollars in debt. Our country is drowning in debt at every level from our personal lives to all of our levels of government, while we don't seem to care.

On January 1, 2018:

- The national debt was $20,597,795,000,000;
- our personal debt was $18,732,681,400,000;
- the state debt was $1,170,906,400,000;
- and the local debt was $1,863,164,000,000.

That is a total government debt of $42,364,546,800,000 which can probably never be repaid.

As you review appendix 4, you will find that since 1956 there has never been any reduction at all. That's 62 years during which the national debt has never been reduced even one penny. We have just kept on borrowing with abandonment.

Note that beginning on the 1st of January 2007 and including up to January 1st 2018 or for 12 years the annual debt of the national government has exceeded $1 trillion 7 times. That is 68.3% of the time. These dates are all during presidencies of President Bush and President Obama, showing that neither of the main political party cares one little bit about the debt.

A significant part of this debt is student debt which totals $1,508,455,000,000. This student debt is ruining the lives of our younger generation because they are beginning their lives in terrible debt. At this time, it seems that this debt can't be avoided because of government and university greed. This debt is accumulating to the point that it probably can never be repaid. It is being held over this generation like a club. Refer to Appendix 5 DVD # 7

All public schools are teaching socialism and a lack of morals so that young people will have little or no moral foundation in their lives. We are running toward the destruction of our nation and its financial future. This will come crashing down around us at some point. It cannot be avoided!

Another factor to include in this discussion is the increase of the money supply that occurs every year. Inflation is tied to the money supply, so every time the national debt increases, the money supply also increases, and inflation grows. In our economy, the debt and the money supply are currently working in tandem. Refer to Appendix 5 DVD # 9

These are some real facts about the national debt:

- When the national debt was created, no actual money ever changed hands. The money was created by underhanded accounting methods.

- There is always interest on debts. The interest on the national debt is paid to the owners of the Federal Reserve that created the money out of nothing.

- The interest is paid in hard earned cash while no actual money was ever loaned when the debt was created.

- We, the people of the United States, never received any money, but it is assumed that we must pay back the principal and the interest on that fake debt.

This is the situation of the national debt. We owe interest and principal on money we never received. Counterfeiters just created it and the government told us it was real money. We have been cheated by our own government elected officials so they could line their pockets out of our misery.

Let's now look at what the national debt really is. Here is one of the definitions from Webster's Dictionary of 1828:

"The notes or bills which are issued by the public or by corporations or individuals, which circulate on the confidence of men in the ability and disposition in those who issue them, to redeem them. They are sometimes called bills of credit."

Therefore, the so called national debt is not a debt at all. It is a bill of credit! Bills of credit do not charge the recipient interest. The creator of the bills of credit pays the interest to the receiver. We are the recipients of these bills of credit. We have been deceived by the substitution of the word debt for bills of credit.

Many of the words that the government uses to control us have had their meanings changed to confuse us. The word substitution of debt for, bills of credit, illustrates this type of deception. The word debt has been used to enslave us by creating in our minds that we are in debt! These Federal Reserve Notes are pure and simply bills of credit. Since all of the money provided to the United States Government since the creation of the Federal Reserve in 1913 is officially called Federal Reserve Notes, they are not debt instruments. We accept and use them on the good faith of the government to reimburse us as pointed out in the definition above. We legally do not owe a debt or any interest on these bills of credit and never have! It has been called a non-debt debt by Jerry Voorhis, a Congressman during the 1940s. Refer to Appendix 5 DVD # 5

In reality all money created through the Federal Reserve is really fiat money or fiat currency. That means the money created out of nothing and backed by nothing. That is why it is a non-debt debt. We are being deceived by the federal government and the Federal Reserve while they profit from the deception.

Socialism vs Capitalism

There is a fierce battle going on today for control of our nation. It is not on the battlefield but rather in our schools at all levels, especially in the colleges and universities. What is this battle about? It is about freedom of choice. In 1776 two opposing forces, freedom-capitalism or slavery-socialism, were officially both started. Both of these forces have existed throughout history and were often in a form of government. In 1776 these forces were official organized with worldwide political influence. One was formed on May 1st and was called the Illuminati, and the other began on July 4th with the acceptance of The Declaration of Independence. Refer to Appendix 5 DVD # 6

What are modern terms used in conjunction with these forces? The one organized on May 1st is socialism and the one organized on July 4th is capitalism. It is interesting that the Illuminati is hidden from the people and if it is ever mentioned by someone, that person is ridiculed as a conspiracy theorist and branded a kook. Ridicule is a tool used to prevent closer inspection of a concept, and since the Illuminati is so well hidden from most people, it is easy to call anyone crazy who even mentions it. While the other side, capitalism, is always out in the open.

There are instances of capitalism when it has been misused. These instances are cases of extremely large capitalistic groups, and they use their power to destroy the freedoms of others. However, we should not lose sight of the fact that it is pure free capitalism that has built this great nation.

Socialism, pure and simple, is just allowing the government to control the society. This control occurs when government passes laws that restrict liberties. A current well known example would be Obamacare. This so called health insurance bill is really just a way for the government to control who receives healthcare and who doesn't. It has hidden rules that require private companies to pay for items that are against their consciences. It has death panels which decide whether or not a person is too old for certain procedures. It has taxes to force citizens to be a part of it even if they cannot afford it. It was not actually passed for healthcare but rather for control of Americans. A government that wants socialism is a government that wants control of its citizens lives. Our Constitution was written to allow people freedom of choice in their lives and socialism destroys that freedom.

There are many countries that have tried to completely implement socialism, but it has always failed. Obvious examples include Russia, Cuba, China, and Venezuela. Each of these countries, including Russia, had an economy of choice, which was destroyed by war or just the selfishness of their government officials. Regardless of the system these countries had prior to socialism, the result of socialism was extreme poverty and death. In each of these cases the government arrested and tortured anyone who disagreed. Murder by government became the rule of law, and the people suffered.

There are also many countries that just slowly advanced toward socialism. Examples of these countries include Sweden, England, and many other Western European countries to a greater or lessor degree. In each of these cases, taxes were raised to pay for the benefits that the government passed out to its citizens.

Margaret Thatcher, a prime minister of England, once said "The trouble with socialism is that eventually you run out of other people's money." It is often felt that the rich have an endless supply of money and, therefore must support the rest of the society. However, the fact is that if you took all of the money the wealthy have, a government would only run for a few weeks.

As you ponder what has happened throughout American history, you will see many ups and downs of our freedoms. President Roosevelt did a masterful job of establishing socialism in our previously free enterprise system, and many of his programs are still with us and growing larger and larger. We must put a stop to this, or we will find ourselves with a completely socialized economy.

What is the foundation of the current socialization of the economies of the world? Socialism, as we know it today, began in the late 1800s. Karl Marx wrote the *Communist Manifesto*, which was published in 1848. It was largely unnoticed until the Fabian Socialist Society took it from obscurity to the forefront. The Fabian Socialist Society was sponsored by Cecil Rhodes who organized the Circle Groups which were the forerunners of the Council on Foreign Relations (CFR) in the United States and the Royal Institute of International Affairs in England. These two organizations were the major factors behind the United Nations which is also a socialistic organization.

We are being controlled by some capitalistic financial individuals who are taking advantage of the greed of citizens to further the goal of worldwide socialism. One of the main tools of this expansion of socialism is the World Economic Forum, which is held each January in Davos, Switzerland. This forum is the one which controls many of the governments of the world. In fact, if the governments would just leave well enough alone, the economies would fix themselves, and we would all be much better off.

Here is an example of what socialism actually does. This example happened in a class of students who had been taught all of the benefits of socialism.

It seems that there was a college with an economics professor who said he had never failed a single student before but had, once, failed an entire class. That class had insisted that socialism worked and that no one would be poor and no one would be rich, a great equalizer or everyone would be equal. The professor then said ok, we will have an experiment in this class on socialism.

All grades will be averaged and everyone would receive the same grade so no one would fail. The students were thrilled. Finally, here is a class that would have no failures. After the first test, the grades were averaged and everyone got a B. The students who studied hard were upset, and the students who studied very little were happy.

Then, as the second test rolled around, the students who studied just a little studied even less and the ones who studied hard decided they also wanted a free ride. Therefore, they didn't study either. The grades on second test averaged a D! No one was happy.

When the 3rd test rolled around the average was an F.

The scores never increased as bickering, blame, name calling all resulted in hard feelings and no one would study for anyone else.

Everyone in the class failed. The professor then told them that socialism would always fail because there was no benefit to do anything to personally succeed. The economic law is this: The greater the reward the more people will try to succeed. When the reward for success is taken away, no one will try or succeed. Many call the benefits of your effort selfishness and it is looked down upon, but it is actually the real creator of the best and wealthiest economic societies.

We've spent a good deal of time on socialism, so let's look at capitalism. Driving down the street in a local city, I saw a sign on a house window proclaiming "End Capitalism." Refer to Appendix 5 DVD # 3

One wonders what that person really wanted. Did he want to close all stores because they sell something and make enough to buy more and pay the help? Did he want to stop people from inventing something and then trying to sell it so they can make more? Just what does that person want.

Before we can end something, we must first know what we are talking about. Are we talking about the items just mentioned? Are we talking about big business that provides us with the food we eat, so we don't have to raise or grow it ourselves? Is the goal of these people to turn back the clock to when we had no conveniences? Maybe, the goal is to do away with our free agency to produce and to try to improve ourselves. Maybe, the goal is to stop all of the world's biggest corporations that are trying to get control of our lives. By the way, socialism is nearly the opposite of capitalism, and socialism is the tool used by those big corporations just mentioned, to control our lives.

So perhaps we should stop for a few minutes and decide what is bad in our lives before we decide to will-nilly end or to stop something. You see capitalism is the liberty to do what you would like to do with your private property. It is free agency. It is being allowed to succeed at something without the government looking over your shoulder and controlling you. In fact, the sign that said "End Capitalism," only existed because that person could make it and display it. In a controlled socialistic society, if the sign said end socialism the state police would be on the scene to destroy that sign and arrest that individual unless he had a permit to display it. In other words, in a socialistic society, you must have government permission to do anything.

What would it be like to live in a society that was devoid of capitalism? First, there would be almost nothing to buy. Nothing new would be invented or discovered. No one would be personally successful at anything because the government would decide what you were to do and would establish quotas that must be met. Those quotas were usually established by people who really don't know what you are doing, with rules that would be almost impossible to achieve. Why is this? It is because those are the people who have risen to the top in a society that controls everything, and they get there by promising the impossible. That is historical and has happened in every society that has tried to do away with capitalism.

Capitalism is the natural way of nature. People want to strive to do better in their lives. They see ways to improve their lot in life and then implement those ideas. It is the natural way of life to want to be better and have more. It is natural to do that, by improving oneself and as everybody improves themselves, the society improves and everyone benefits. These benefits occur because each individual thinks of new and better ways of living, and each idea from each person is different. Every person is different, and when capitalism puts all of these different individuals together, and each tries his best to improve himself, everyone is benefited and the society improves as a whole. That is the natural way of things, and it always works in that direction.

Everything that we have today, we have because someone thought of it and then did it, to better himself. He wasn't concerned about others just himself. That "selfish concern" provided that item to everyone in the society and all benefited.

As society gets more and more complicated, the new products and services become more complicated requiring people to form and finance companies to make and provide these items. That is capitalism. Without capitalism, none of our conveniences would ever have been produced. They would not be available to us, because even if they had been thought of, there would have been no way to produce them. Without capitalism that sign on that house window could not have been made, as the material of the sign itself would never have been produced. The paint used for the letters would not have been available either. The house that held up the sign would never have been built, as the materials required to build it would never have been made. Therefore, if capitalism had ended 2 or 3 hundred years ago, he would be living in a shack built out of tree limbs and covered with leaves, as nothing better would have ever been provided.

Therefore, it would be better to ponder what life would be like, if we had never had capitalism, before we try to destroy it. Maybe, we would be just destroying our own futures.

As mentioned above people sometimes say capitalism breeds selfishness. Why? When we do better than someone else, it does not take away their opportunity to do the same thing or something else, and if we all did better things for ourselves, then society would be better. That is capitalism! Why is it selfish?

Those who defame selfishness usually want something. It all comes down to "I want something but I'm not willing to do the effort to have it." Therefore, others who do the effort and have something are selfish. The concept of having the government take something from someone and give it to someone else is simply government theft. Envy and covertness create theft either individually or by government. Some say those that have something they can't have, are selfish, but it is really just childishly taking from someone, things which you want.

Recently the pope said some nice things about the poor and recommended ditching capitalism for socialism to help the poor. But the end result of that recommendation would be more poverty, suffering, and death.

John M. Keynes believed that capitalism or free enterprise would never result in full employment, and he was right. Capitalism would never result in full employment, but neither capitalism nor socialism provide full employment. When the government has tried to get full employment using socialism and deficit spending, inflation has always been the result.

Capitalism is the tool that provides for a successful economy, while socialism provides poverty, control and a loss of freedom.

Appendix 1

The following item covers how economics and liberty flow together, as each are a part of the other, and how the best economic opportunities result from the complete economic freedom allowed by the best type of government, which is a Republic, which is the basis of our Constitution.

Here is an example of what is required for the production of one of the most basic items, the pencil.

I, Pencil

By Leonard E. Read
Are We Good Enough for Liberty?
by Lawrence W. Reed
Pages 39-47
Foundation for Economic Education (FEE)

"I am a lead pencil - the ordinary wooden pencil familiar to all boys and girls and adults who can read and write.

"Writing is both my vocation and my avocation; that's all I do.

"You may wonder why I should write a genealogy. Well, to begin with, my story is interesting. And, next, I am a mystery - more so than a tree or a sunset or even a flash of lightening. But, sadly, I am taken for granted by those who use me, as if I were a mere incident and without background.

This supercilious attitude relegates me to the level of the commonplace. This is a species of grievous error in which mankind cannot too long persist without peril. For, the wise GK. Chesterton observed, "We are perishing for want of wonder, not for want of wonders."

"I, Pencil, simple though I appear to be, merit your wonder and awe, a claim I shall attempt to prove. In fact, if you can understand me - no, that's too much to ask of anyone - if you can become aware of the miraculousness which I symbolize, you can help save the freedom mankind is so unhappily losing. I have a profound lesson to teach, and I can teach this lesson better than can an automobile or an airplane or a mechanical dishwasher because - well, because I am seemingly so simple.

"Simple? Yet, not a single person on the face of this earth knows how to make me. This sounds fantastic, doesn't it? Especially when it is realized that there are about one and one-half billion of my kind produced in the United States each year.

"Pick me up and look me over. What do you see? Not much meets the eye - there's some wood, lacquer, the printed labeling, graphite lead, a bit of metal, and an eraser.

Innumerable Antecedents

"Just as you cannot trace your family tree back very far, so it is impossible for me to name and explain all my antecedents. But I would like to suggest enough of them to impress upon you the richness and complexity of my background.

"My family tree begins with what in fact is a tree, a cedar of straight grain that grows in Northern California and Oregon. Now contemplate all the saws and trucks and rope and the countless other gear used in harvesting and carting the cedar logs to the railroad siding. Think of all the persons and the numberless skills that went into their fabrication: the mining of ore, the making of steel and its refinement into saws, axes, motors; the growing of hemp and bringing it through all of the stages to heavy and strong rope; the logging camps with their beds and mess halls, the cookery and the raising of all the foods. Why, untold thousands of persons had a hand in every cup of coffee the loggers drink!

"The logs are shipped to a mill in San Leandro, California. Can you imagine the individuals who make flat cars and rails and railroad engines and who construct and install the communications systems incidental thereto? Those legions are among my antecedents.

"Consider the millwork in San Leandro. The cedar logs are cut into small, pencil-length slats less than one-fourth of an inch in thickness. These are kiln dried and then tinted for the same reason women put rouge on their faces. People prefer that I look pretty, not a pallid white. The slats are waxed and kiln dried again. How many skills went into the

129

making of the tint and the kilns, into supplying the heat, the light and power, the belts, motors, and all the other things a mill requires? Are sweepers in the mill among my ancestors? Yes, and included are the men who poured the concrete for the dam of a Pacific Gas & Electric Company hydro plant which supplies the mill's power.

"Don't overlook the ancestors present and distant who have a hand in transporting sixty cartloads of slats across the nation.

"Once in the pencil factory - $4,000,000 in machinery and buildings, all capital accumulated by thrifty and saving parents of mine - each slat is given eight grooves by a complex machine, after which another machine lays leads in every other slat, applies glue, and places another slat atop - a lead sandwich, so to speak. Seven brothers and I are mechanically carved from the "wood-clinched" sandwich.

"My "lead" itself - it contains no lead at all - is complex. The graphite is mined in Ceylon [Sri Lanka]. Consider these miners and those who make their many tools and the makers of the paper sacks in which the graphite is shipped and those who make the string that ties the sacks and those who put them aboard ships and those who make the ships. Even the lighthouse keepers along the way assisted in my birth - and the harbor pilots.

"The graphite is mixed with clay from Mississippi in which ammonium hydroxide is used in the refining process. Then wetting agents are added such as sulfonated tallow - animal fats chemically reacted with sulfuric acid. After passing through numerous machines, the mixture finally appears as endless extrusions, - as from a sausage grinder - cut to size, dried, and baked for several hours at 1,850 degrees Fahrenheit. To increase their strength and smoothness the leads are then treated with a hot mixture which includes candelilla wax from Mexico, paraffin wax, and hydrogenated natural fats.

"My cedar receives six coats of lacquer. Do you know all of the ingredients of lacquer? Who would think that the growers of castor beans and the refiners of castor oil are a part of it? They are. Why, even the processes by which the lacquer is made a beautiful yellow involve the skills of more persons than one can enumerate!

"Observe the labeling. That's a film formed by applying heat to carbon black mixed with resins. How do you make resins and what, pray, is carbon black?

"My bit of metal - the ferrule - is brass. Think of all the persons who mine zinc and copper and those who have the skills to make shiny sheet brass from these products of nature. Those black rings on my ferrule are black nickel. What is black nickel and how is it applied? The complete story of why the center of my ferrule has no black nickel on it would take pages to explain.

"Then there's my crowning glory, inelegantly referred to in the trade as "the plug," the part man uses to erase the errors he makes with me. An ingredient called "factice" is what does the erasing. It is a rubber-like product made by reacting rapeseed oil from the Dutch East Indies [Indonesia] with sulfur chloride. Rubber, contrary to the common notion, is only for binding purposes. Then, too, there are numerous vulcanizing and accelerating agents. The pumice comes from Italy; and the pigment which gives "the plug" its color is cadmium sulfide.

No one Knows

"Does anyone wish to challenge my earlier assertion that no single person on the face of this earth knows how to make me?

"Actually, millions of human beings have had a hand in my creation, no one of whom even knows more than a few of the others. Now you may say that I go too far in relating the picker of a coffee berry in far-off Brazil and food growers elsewhere to my creation; that this is an extreme position. I shall stand by my claim. There isn't a single person in all these millions, including the president of the pencil company, who contributes more than a tiny, infinitesimal bit of know-how. From the standpoint of know how the only difference between the miner of graphite in Ceylon and the logger in Oregon is in the type of know-how. Neither the miner nor the logger can be dispensed with, any more than can the chemist at the factory or the worker in the oil field - paraffin being a byproduct of petroleum.

"Here is an astounding fact: Neither the worker in the oil field nor the chemist nor the digger of graphite or clay nor any who mans or makes the ships or trains or trucks nor the one who runs the machine that does the knurling on my bit of metal nor the president of the company performs his singular task because he wants me. Each one wants me less, perhaps, than does a child in the first grade. Indeed, there are some among this vast multitude who never saw a pencil nor would they know how to use one. Their motivation is other than me. Perhaps it is something like this: Each of these millions sees that he can thus exchange his tiny know how for the goods and services he needs or wants. I may or may not be among these items.

No Master Mind

"There is a fact still more astounding: the absence of a master mind, of anyone dictating or forcibly directing these countless actions which bring me into being. No trace of such a person can be found. Instead, we find the Invisible Hand at work. This is the mystery to which I earlier referred.

"It has been said that "only God can make a tree." Why do we agree with this? Isn't it because we realize that we ourselves could not make one?

Indeed, can we even describe a tree? We cannot, except in superficial terms. We can say, for instance, that a certain molecular configuration manifests itself as a tree. But what mind is there among men that could even record, let alone direct, the constant changes in molecules that transpire in the life span of a tree? Such a feat is utterly unthinkable!

"I, Pencil, am a complex combination of miracles: a tree, zinc, copper, graphite, and so on. But to these miracles which manifest themselves in nature an even more extraordinary miracle has been added: the configuration of creative human energies, millions of tiny know hows configurating naturally and spontaneously in response to human necessity and desire and in the absence of any human masterminding! Since only God can make a tree, I insist that only God could make me. Men can no more direct these millions of know hows to bring me into being than he can put molecules together to create a tree.

"The above is what I meant when writing, "If you can become aware of the miraculousness which I symbolize, you can help save the freedom mankind is so unhappily losing." For, if one is aware that these know hows will naturally, yes, automatically, arrange themselves into creative and productive patterns in response to human necessity and demand, that is, in the absence of governmental or any other coercive master-minding, then one will possess an absolutely essential ingredient for freedom: a faith in free people. Freedom is impossible without this faith.

"Once government has had a monopoly of a creative activity such, for instance, as the delivery of the mails, most individuals will believe that the mail could not be efficiently delivered by men acting freely. And here is the reason: Each one acknowledges that he himself doesn't know how to do all of the things incident to mail delivery. He also recognizes that no other individual could do it. These assumptions are correct. No individual possesses enough know how to perform a nation's mail delivery any more than any individual possesses enough know now to make a pencil. Now, in the absence of faith in free people, in the unawareness that millions of tiny know hows would naturally and miraculously form and cooperate to satisfy this necessity, the individual cannot help but reach the erroneous conclusion that mail can be delivered only be governmental "masterminding.""

Testimony Galore

"If I, Pencil, were the only item that could offer testimony on what men and women can accomplish when free to try, then those with little faith would have a fair case. However, there is testimony galore; it's all about us and on every hand. Mail delivery is exceedingly simple when compared, for instance, to the making of an automobile or a calculating machine or a grain combine or a milling machine or to tens of thousands of other things. Delivery? Why, in this area where men have been left free to try, they deliver the human voice around the world in less than one second; they deliver an event visually and in motion to any person's home when it is happening; they deliver 150 passengers from Seattle to Baltimore in less than four hours; they deliver gas from Texas to one's range or furnace in New York at unbelievably low rates and without subsidy; they deliver each four pounds of oil from the Persian Gulf to our Eastern Seaboard, halfway around the world, for less money than the government charges for delivering a one-ounce letter across the street!

"The lesson I have to teach is this: Leave all creative energies uninhibited. Merely organize society to act in harmony with this lesson. Let society's legal apparatus remove all obstacles the best it can. Permit these creative know hows freely to flow. Have faith that free men and women will respond to the Invisible Hand. This faith will be confirmed. I, Pencil, seemingly simple though I am, offer the miracle of my creation as testimony that this is a practical faith, as practical as the sun, the rain, a cedar tree, the good earth.

Appendix 2

Money Supply

Before you look at the numbers, you need to know what they mean. Simply and basically M1 signifies the money you carry around in your pocket, the money in your checking account, the money in your saving account. In other words, M1 is the actual money we see and use. M2 is the money represented by credit cards and other small loans. M3 consists of the large loans of $100,000 or more along with the dollars that are used overseas: European dollars. They are not Euros, but Eurodollars, and it is American money used exclusively overseas, never in the United States. However, even though we never see it in our country, it still effects what the prices of goods and services will be in our country. Inflation is caused by the total money supply increasing. The more the supply of money increases, the greater the inflation. All numbers in the chart represent billions of dollars.

Chart of the Money Supply from 1931 to 2006

Year	1931				1932		
	Jan	Apr	Jul	Oct	Jan	Apr	Jul
Grand T	24.4	23.6	23.1	21.6	20.9	20.3	21.0
Margin	(0.1)	(0.8)	(0.5)	(1.5)	(0.7)	(0.6)	.7
M3 Total							
Margin M3							
M1/M3							
M1 Total	24.4	23.6	23.1	21.6	20.9	20.3	21.0
Margin M1	(0.1)	(0.8)	(0.5)	(1.5)	(0.7)	(0.6)	.7
M2 Total							
Margin M2							
	Jan	Apr	Jul	Oct	Jan	Apr	Jul
Year	1931				1932		

Daily Treasury Statements
Federal Reserve Statistical Releases

Year		1933				1934	
	Oct	Jan	Apr	Jul	Oct	Jan	Apr
Grand T	20.2	18.9	19.1	19.0	19.6	20.6	20.9
Margin	(0.8)	(1.3)	0.2	(0.1)	0.6	1.0	0.3
M3 Total							
Margin M3							
M1/M3							
M1 Total	20.2	18.9	19.1	19.0	19.6	20.6	20.9
Margin M1	(0.8)	(1.3)	0.2	(0.1)	0.6	1.0	0.3
M2 Total							
Margin M2							
	Oct	Jan	Apr	Jul	Oct	Jan	Apr
Year		1933				1934	

Daily Treasury Statements
Federal Reserve Statistical Releases

Year			1935				1936
	Jul	Oct	Jan	Apr	Jul	Oct	Jan
Grand T	21.9	22.6	24.0	25.0	26.1	26.8	27.3
Margin	1.0	0.7	1.4	1.0	1.1	0.7	0.5
M3 Total							
Margin M3							
M1/M3							
M1 Total	21.9	22.6	24.0	25.0	26.1	26.8	27.3
Margin M1	1.0	0.7	1.4	1.0	1.1	0.7	0.5
M2 Total							
Margin M2							
	Jul	Oct	Jan	Apr	Jul	Oct	Jan
Year			1935				1936

Daily Treasury Statements
Federal Reserve Statistical Releases

Year				1937			
	Apr	Jul	Oct	Jan	Apr	Jul	Oct
Grand T	29.3	29.8	30.5	30.7	30.2	29.8	28.8
Margin	2.0	0.5	0.7	0.2	(0.4)	(1.0)	(1.0)
M3 Total							
Margin M3							
M1/M3							
M1 Total	29.3	29.8	30.5	30.7	30.2	29.8	28.8
Margin M1	2.0	0.5	0.7	0.2	(0.5)	(0.4)	(1.0)
M2 Total							
Margin M2							
	Apr	Jul	Oct	Jan	Apr	Jul	Oct
Year				1937			

Daily Treasury Statements
Federal Reserve Statistical Releases

Year	1938				1939		
	Jan	Apr	Jul	Oct	Jan	Apr	Jul
Grand To	29.3	28.9	30.3	31.4	31.7	32.3	34.8
Margin	0.5	(0.4)	1.4	1.1	0.3	0.6	2.5
M3 Total							
Margin M3							
M1/M3							
M1 Total	29.3	28.9	30.3	31.4	31.7	32.3	34.8
Margin M1	0.5	(0.4)	1.4	1.1	0.3	0.6	2.5
M2 Total							
Margin M2							
	Jan	Apr	Jul	Oct	Jan	Apr	Jul
Year	1938				1939		

Daily Treasury Statements
Federal Reserve Statistical Releases

Year		1940				1941	
	Oct	Jan	Apr	Jul	Oct	Jan	Apr
Grand To	36.8	37.3	38.6	39.7	41.6	44.1	45.0
Margin	2.0	0.5	1.3	1.1	1.9	2.5	0.9
M3 Total							
Margin M3							
M1/M3							
M1 Total	36.8	37.3	38.6	39.7	41.6	44.1	45.0
Margin M1	2.0	0.5	1.3	1.1	1.9	2.5	0.9
M2 Total							
Margin M2							
	Oct	Jan	Apr	Jul	Oct	Jan	Apr
Year		1940				1941	

Daily Treasury Statements
Federal Reserve Statistical Releases

Year			1942				1943
	Jul	Oct	Jan	Apr	Jul	Oct	Jan
Grand To	46.7	47.6	50.0	52.5	57.0	61.5	67.8
Margin	1.7	0.9	2.4	2.5	4.5	4.5	6.3
M3 Total							
Margin M3							
M1/M3							
M1 Total	46.7	47.6	50.0	52.5	57.0	61.5	67.8
Margin M1	1.7	0.9	2.4	2.5	4.5	4.5	6.3
M2 Total							
Margin M2							
	Jul	Oct	Jan	Apr	Jul	Oct	Jan
Year			1942				1943

Daily Treasury Statements
Federal Reserve Statistical Releases

Year				1944			
	Apr	Jul	Oct	Jan	Apr	Jul	Oct
Grand To	71.4	70.5	78.1	78.9	81.4	86.3	88.6
Margin	3.6	(0.9)	7.6	0.8	2.5	4.9	2.3
M3 Total							
Margin M3							
M1/M3							
M1 Total	71.4	70.5	78.1	78.9	81.4	86.3	88.6
Margin M1	3.6	(0.9)	7.6	0.8	2.5	4.9	2.3
M2 Total							
Margin M2							
	Apr	Jul	Oct	Jan	Apr	Jul	Oct
Year				1944			

Daily Treasury Statements
Federal Reserve Statistical Releases

Year	1945				1946		
	Jan	Apr	Jul	Oct	Jan	Apr	Jul
Grand To	94.9	95.2	99.4	100.0	100.5	104.4	105.3
Margin	6.3	0.3	4.2	0.6	0.5	3.9	0.9
M3 Total							
Margin M3							
M1/M3							
M1 Total	94.9	95.2	99.4	100.0	100.5	104.4	105.3
Margin M1	6.3	0.3	4.2	0.6	0.5	3.9	0.9
M2 Total							
Margin M2							
	Jan	Apr	Jul	Oct	Jan	Apr	Jul
Year	1945				1946		

Daily Treasury Statements
Federal Reserve Statistical Releases

Year	1947				1948		
	Oct	Jan	Apr	Jul	Oct	Jan	Apr
Grand T	105.2	107.1	108.7	109.7	108.9	172.2	172.1
Margin	(0.1)	1.9	1.6	1.0	(0.8)	??	(0.1)
M3 Total						1.3	1.3
Margin M3						??	0
M1/M3							83.54
M1 Tota	105.2	107.1	108.7	109.7	108.9	109.3	108.6
Margi M1	(0.1)	1.9	1.6	1.0	(0.8)	0.4	(0.7)
M2 Total						61.6	62.2
Margin M2						??	0.6
	Oct	Jan	Apr	Jul	Oct	Jan	Apr
Year	1947					1948	

Daily Treasury Statements
Federal Reserve Statistical Releases

Year			1949			
	Jul	Oct	Jan	Apr	Jul	Oct
Grand To	173.1	173.1	173.4	174.3	174.5	175.3
Margin	1.0	0.0	0.3	0.9	0.2	0.8
M3 Total	1.4	1.4	1.4	1.4	1.3	1.4
Margin M3	0.1	0.0	0.0	0.	(0.1)	0.1
M1/M3	77.79	77.43	77.14	77.07	82.7	77.07
M1 Total	108.9	108.4	108.0	107.9	107.6	107.9
Margin M1	0.3	(0.5)	(0.4)	(0.1)	(0.3)	0.3
M2 Total	62.8	63.3	64.0	65.0	65.6	66.0
Margin M2	0.6	0.5	0.7	1.0	0.6	0.4
	Jul	Oct	Jan	Apr	Jul	Oct
Year			1949			

Daily Treasury Statements
Federal Reserve Statistical Releases

Year	1950				1951	
	Jan	Apr	Jul	Oct	Jan	Apr
Grand To	177.6	180.2	181.3	183.1	184.8	186.7
Margin	2.3	2.6	1.1	1.8	1.7	1.9
M3 Total	1.4	1.5	1.4	1.5	1.5	1.4
Margin M3	0.0	0.1	(0.1)	0.1	0.0	(0.1)
M1/M3	78.00	73.80	79.93	75.33	76.20	82.29
M1 Total	109.2	110.7	111.9	113.0	114.3	115.2
Margin M1	1.3	1.5	1.2	1.1	1.3	0.9
M2 Total	67.0	68.0	68.0	68.2	69.0	70.1
Margin M2	1.0	1.0	0.0	0.6	0.4	1.1
	Jan	Apr	Jul	Oct	Jan	Apr
Year	1950				1951	

Daily Treasury Statements
Federal Reserve Statistical Releases

Year			1952			
	Jul	Oct	Jan	Apr	Jul	Oct
Grand To	190.1	194.0	197.3	200.2	203.6	206.9
Margin	3.4	3.9	3.3	2.9	3.4	3.3
M3 Total	1.5	1.5	1.6	1.6	1.6	1.7
Margin M3	0.1	0.0	0.1	0.0	0.0	0.1
M1/M3	78.00	79.60	75.38	76.12	76.88	73.12
M1 Total	117.0	119.4	120.6	121.8	123.0	124.3
Margin M1	1.8	2.4	1.2	1.2	1.2	1.3
M2 Total	71.6	73.1	75.1	76.8	79.0	80.9
Margin M2	1.5	1.5	2.0	1.7	2.2	1.9
	Jul	Oct	Jan	Apr	Jul	Oct
Year			1952			

Daily Treasury Statements
Federal Reserve Statistical Releases

Year	1953				1954	
	Jan	Apr	Jul	Oct	Jan	Apr
Grand To	209.6	212.1	214.7	217.4	220.4	223.8
Margin	2.7	2.5	2.6	2.7	3.0	3.4
M3 Total	1.7	1.7	1.7	1.7	1.8	1.8
Margin M3	0.0	0.0	0.0	0.0	0.1	0.0
M1/M3	73.35	73.59	73.71	73.88	69.94	70.28
M1 Total	124.7	125.1	125.3	125.6	125.9	126.5
Margin M1	0.4	0.4	0.2	0.3	0.3	0.6
M2 Total	82.2	85.3	87.7	90.1	92.7	95.5
Margin M2	2.3	2.1	2.4	2.4	2.6	2.8
	Jan	Apr	Jul	Oct	Jan	Apr
Year	1953				1954	

Daily Treasury Statements
Federal Reserve Statistical Releases

Year			1955			
	Jul	Oct	Jan	Apr	Jul	Oct
Grand To	227.6	231.2	234.6	237.6	240.2	242.9
Margin	3.8	3.6	3.4	3.0	2.6	2.7
M3 Total	1.8	1.8	1.8	1.9	1.8	2.0
Margin M3	0.0	0.0	0.0	0.1	(0.1)	0.2
M1/M3	70.89	71.72	72.33	69.00	73.17	66.00
M1 Total	127.6	129.1	130.2	131.1	131.7	132.0
Margin M1	1.1	1.5	1.1	0.9	0.6	0.3
M2 Total	98.2	100.3	102.6	104.6	106.7	108.9
Margin M2	2.7	2.1	2.3	2.0	2.1	2.2
	Jul	Oct	Jan	Apr	Jul	Oct
Year			1955			

Daily Treasury Statements
Federal Reserve Statistical Releases

Year	1956				1957	
	Jan	Apr	Jul	Oct	Jan	Apr
Grand To	245.1	247.8	250.6	253.6	257.0	259.8
Margin	2.2	2.7	2.8	3.0	3.4	2.8
M3 Total	1.9	2.0	2.0	2.0	2.1	2.0
Margin M3	(0.1)	0.1	0.0	0.0	0.1	(0.1)
M1/M3	69.68	66.35	66.45	66.85	63.62	66.80
M1 Total	132.4	132.7	132.9	133.7	133.6	133.6
Margin M1	0.4	0.3	0.2	0.8	(0.1)	0.0
M2 Total	110.8	113.1	115.7	117.9	121.3	124.2
Margin M2	0.4	0.3	0.2	0.8	0.1	0.0
	Jan	Apr	Jul	Oct	Jan	Apr
Year	1956				1957	

Daily Treasury Statements
Federal Reserve Statistical Releases

Year			1958			
	Jul	Oct	Jan	Apr	Jul	Oct
Grand To	262.5	264.9	270.3	277.0	282.0	286.5
Margin	2.7	2.4	5.4	6.7	5.0	4.5
M3 Total	2.1	2.1	2.2	2.2	2.2	2.3
Margin M3	0.1	0.0	0.1	0.0	0.0	0.1
M1/M3	63.52	63.19	60.55	61.41	61.96	60.00
M1 Total	133.4	132.7	133.2	135.1	136.3	138.0
Margin M1	(0.2)	(0.7)	(0.5)	(0.1)	1.2	1.7
M2 Total	127.0	130.1	134.9	139.7	143.5	146.2
Margin M2	2.8	3.1	4.8	4.8	3.8	2.7
	Jul	Oct	Jan	Apr	Jul	Oct
Year			1958			

Daily Treasury Statements
Federal Reserve Statistical Releases

Year	1959				1960	
	Jan	Apr	Jul	Oct	Jan	Apr
Grand To	292.0	292.5	296.7	298.9	303.4	302.4
Margin	5.5	0.5	4.2	2.2	4.5	(0.1)
M3 Total	2.2	2.3	2.3	2.0	1.9	2.1
Margin M3	(0.1)	0.1	0.0	(0.3)	(0.1)	0.2
M1/M3	64.64	60.74	61.00	70.35	75.42	66.52
M1 Total	142.2	139.7	140.3	140.7	143.3	139.7
Margin M1	4.2	(2.5)	0.6	0.4	2.6	(3.6)
M2 Total	147.6	150.5	154.1	156.2	158.2	160.6
Margin M2	1.4	2.9	3.6	2.1	2.0	2.4
	Jan	Apr	Jul	Oct	Jan	Apr
Year	1959				1960	

Daily Treasury Statements
Federal Reserve Statistical Releases

Year			1961			
	Jul	Oct	Jan	Apr	Jul	Oct
Grand To	305.8	312.5	320.5	324.2	330.0	336.8
Margin	3.4	6.7	8.0	3.7	5.8	6.8
M3 Total	2.3	2.6	3.0	4.0	5.1	5.3
Margin M3	0.2	0.3	0.4	1.0	1.1	0.2
M1/M3	60.39	54.31	48.17	35.60	27.75	27.25
M1 Total	138.9	141.2	144.5	142.4	141.5	144.4
Margin M1	(0.8)	2.3	3.3	(2.1)	(0.9)	2.9
M2 Total	164.6	168.7	173.0	177.8	183.4	187.1
Margin M2	4.0	4.1	4.3	4.8	5.6	3.7
	Jul	Oct	Jan	Apr	Jul	Oct
Year			1961			

Daily Treasury Statements
Federal Reserve Statistical Releases

Year	1962				1963	
	Jan	Apr	Jul	Oct	Jan	Apr
Grand To	346.5	352.7	357.4	365.3	377.9	383.9
Margin	9.7	6.2	4.7	7.9	12.6	6.0
M3 Total	5.4	6.7	7.3	7.8	8.8	10.1
Margin M3	0.1	1.3	0.6	0.5	1.0	1.3
M1/M3	27.57	21.90	19.86	18.85	17.28	14.85
M1 Total	148.9	146.7	145.0	147.0	152.1	150.0
Margin M1	4.5	(2.2)	(1.7)	2.0	5.1	(2.1)
M2 Total	192.2	199.3	205.1	210.2	217.0	223.8
Margin M2	5.1	7.1	5.8	5.4	6.5	6.8
	Jan	Apr	Jul	Oct	Jan	Apr
Year	1962				1963	

Daily Treasury Statements
Federal Reserve Statistical Releases

157

Year			1964			
	Jul	Oct	Jan	Apr	Jul	Oct
Grand To	390.9	400.1	412.6	416.8	424.9	436.2
Margin	7.0	9.2	12.5	4.2	8.1	11.3
M3 Total	10.7	11.3	13.0	14.4	15.6	16.3
Margin M3	0.6	0.6	1.7	1.4	1.2	0.7
M1/M3	14.01	13.52	12.15	10.78	9.97	9.80
M1 Total	149.9	152.8	157.9	155.2	155.5	159.7
Margin M1	(0.1)	2.9	5.1	(2.7)	0.3	4.2
M2 Total	230.3	236.0	241.7	247.2	253.8	260.2
Margin M2	6.5	5.7	5.7	5.5	6.6	6.4
	Jul	Oct	Jan	Apr	Jul	Oct
Year			1964			

Daily Treasury Statements
Federal Reserve Statistical Releases

Year	1965				1966	
	Jan	Apr	Jul	Oct	Jan	Apr
Grand To	450.5	455.7	162.6	475.4	490.1	495.3
Margin	14.3	5.2	6.9	12.8	14.7	5.2
M3 Total	18.2	19.5	20.5	21.8	23.0	25.2
Margin M3	1.9	1.3	1.0	1.3	1.2	2.2
M1/M3	9.08	8.34	7.89	7.64	7.56	6.84
M1 Total	165.3	162.6	161.8	166.5	173.8	172.4
Margin M1	5.6	(2.7)	(0.8)	4.7	7.3	(1.4)
M2 Total	267.0	273.6	280.3	287.1	293.3	297.7
Margin M2	6.8	6.6	6.7	6.8	6.2	4.4
	Jan	Apr	Jul	Oct	Jan	Apr
Year	1965				1966	

Daily Treasury Statements
Federal Reserve Statistical Releases

Year			1967			
	Jul	Oct	Jan	Apr	Jul	Oct
Grand To	497.2	502.0	513.7	523.8	537.3	550.8
Margin	1.9	4.8	11.7	10.1	13.5	13.5
M3 Total	26.9	25.1	27.3	30.9	31.1	31.5
Margin M3	1.7	(1.8)	2.2	3.6	0.2	0.4
M1/M3	6.29	6.84	6.47	5.65	5.70	5.78
M1 Total	165.3	162.6	176.6	174.7	177.2	181.9
Margin M1	5.6	(2.7)	5.0	(1.9)	2.5	4.7
M2 Total	301.1	305.3	309.8	318.2	329.0	337.4
Margin M2	6.8	6.6	4.5	8.4	10.8	8.4
	Jul	Oct	Jan	Apr	Jul	Oct
Year			1967			

Daily Treasury Statements
Federal Reserve Statistical Releases

Year	1968				1969	
	Jan	Apr	Jul	Oct	Jan	Apr
Grand To	564.7	570.5	580.7	596.4	612.1	613.2
Margin	13.9	5.8	10.2	15.7	15.7	1.1
M3 Total	32.8	33.6	34.5	37.9	38.6	35.8
Margin M3	1.3	0.8	0.9	3.4	0.7	(2.8)
M1/M3	5.77	5.57	5.50	5.12	5.28	5.63
M1 Total	189.2	187.3	189.8	194.2	203.8	201.5
Margin M1	7.3	(1.9)	2.5	4.4	9.6	(2.3)
M2 Total	342.7	349.6	356.4	364.3	369.7	375.9
Margin M2	5.3	6.9	6.8	7.9	5.4	6.2
	Jan	Apr	Jul	Oct	Jan	Apr
Year	1968				1969	

Daily Treasury Statements
Federal Reserve Statistical Releases

Year			1970			
	Jul	Oct	Jan	Apr	Jun	Oct
Grand To	610.7	609.3	618.3	624.2	637.1	660.5
Margin	(2.5)	(1.4)	9.0	5.9	12.9	23.4
M3 Total	30.1	25.6	26.3	31.3	35.9	46.5
Margin M3	(5.7)	(4.5)	0.7	5.0	4.6	10.6
M1/M3	6.68	7.93	8.02	6.65	5.80	4.57
M1 Total	201.2	202.9	210.8	208.1	208.1	212.3
Margin M1	(0.3)	1.7	7.9	(2.7)	0.0	4.2
M2 Total	379.4	380.8	381.2	384.8	393.1	401.7
Margin M2	3.5	1.4	0.4	3.6	8.3	8.6
	Jul	Oct	Jan	Apr	Jul	Oct
Year			1970			

Daily Treasury Statements
Federal Reserve Statistical Releases

Year	1971				1972	
	Jan	Apr	Jul	Oct	Jan	Apr
Grand To	688.4	718.9	739.8	758.3	786.1	813.2
Margin	27.9	30.5	20.9	18.5	27.8	27.1
M3 Total	52.9	55.4	57.5	62.7	66.1	69.4
Margin M3	6.4	2.5	2.1	5.2	3.4	3.3
M1/M3	4.17	4.00	3.91	3.61	3.56	3.41
M1 Total	220.4	221.4	225.1	226.6	235.0	236.9
Margin M1	8.1	1.0	3.7	1.5	8.4	1.9
M2 Total	415.1	442.1	457.2	469.0	485.0	506.9
Margin M2	13.4	27.0	15.1	11.8	16.0	21.9
	Jan	Apr	Jul	Oct	Jan	Apr
Year	1971				1972	

Daily Treasury Statements
Federal Reserve Statistical Releases

Year			1973			
	Jul	Oct	Jan	Apr	Jul	Oct
Grand To	837.8	863.6	897.8	927.8	953.2	970.2
Margin	24.6	25.8	34.2	30.0	25.4	17.0
M3 Total	74.8	80.0	85.5	102.4	112.5	130.9
Margin M3	5.4	5.2	5.5	16.9	10.1	18.4
M1/M3	3.20	3.05	3.0	2.48	2.3	2.0
M1 Total	236.1	244.2	256.4	254.0	258.1	258.3
Margin M1	2.2	5.1	12.2	(2.4)	4.1	0.2
M2 Total	523.9	539.4	555.9	571.4	582.6	581.0
Margin M2	17.0	15.5	16.5	15.5	11.2	(1.6)
	Jul	Oct	Jan	Apr	Jul	Oct
Year			1973			

Daily Treasury Statements
Federal Reserve Statistical Releases

Year	1974				1975	
	Jan	Apr	Jul	Oct	Jan	Apr
Grand To	994.6	1025.6	1047.3	1057.2	1076.8	1100.8
Margin	24.4	31.0	21.7	9.9	19.6	24.0
M3 Total	133.1	147.0	161.3	166.8	168.8	159.7
Margin M3	2.2	13.9	14.3	5.5	2.0	(9.1)
M1/M3	2.02	1.83	1.68	1.63	1.65	1.74
M1 Total	268.6	268.5	270.1	271.7	278.5	277.7
Margin M1	10.3	(0.1)	1.6	1.6	6.8	(0.8)
M2 Total	592.9	610.1	615.9	618.7	629.5	663.4
Margin M2	11.9	17.2	5.8	2.8	10.8	33.9
	Jan	Apr	Jul	Oct	Jan	Apr
Year	1974				1975	

Daily Treasury Statements
Federal Reserve Statistical Releases

Year			1976			
	Jul	Oct	Jan	Apr	Jul	Oct
Grand T	1131.9	1151.8	1183.2	1221.7	1249.9	1280.4
Margin	31.1	19.9	31.4	38.4	28.2	30.5
M3 Total	152.2	156.2	154.9	154.8	158.3	155.3
Margin M3	(7.5)	4.0	(1.3)	(0.1)	3.5	(3.0)
M1/M3	1.87	1.82	1.89	1.91	1.89	1.95
M1 Total	284.4	284.9	293.2	296.1	298.4	302.9
Margin M1	6.7	0.5	8.3	2.9	2.3	4.5
M2 Total	695.3	710.1	735.1	770.1	793.2	822.2
Margin M2	31.9	15.4	24.4	35.7	22.4	29.0
	Jul	Oct	Jan	Apr	Jul	Oct
Year			1976			

Daily Treasury Statements
Federal Reserve Statistical Releases

Year	1977				1978	
	Jan	Apr	Jul	Oct	Jan	Apr
Grand T	1324.6	1366.2	1405.2	1442.8	1488.9	1633.1
Margin	44.2	41.6	39.0	37.6	46.1	44.2
M3 Total	157.1	159.6	172.3	183.9	206.6	225.7
Margin M3	1.8	2.5	12.7	14.6	19.7	19.1
M1/M3	2.00	2.00	1.87	1.75	1.64	1.52
M1 Total	313.6	318.6	322.2	327.9	339.3	343.4
Margin M1	10.7	5.0	3.6	5.7	11.4	4.1
M2 Total	853.9	888.0	910.7	928.0	943.0	964.0
Margin M2	31.7	34.1	22.7	17.3	15.0	21.0
	Jan	Apr	Jul	Oct	Jan	Apr
Year	1977				1978	

Daily Treasury Statements
Federal Reserve Statistical Releases

Year			1979			
	Jul	Oct	Jan	Apr	Jul	Oct
Grand T	1571.2	1612.9	1660.6	1703.7	1746.6	1798.4
Margin	38.1	41.7	47.7	43.1	42.9	51.8
M3 Total	241.1	257.6	285.4	295.3	307.3	334.8
Margin M3	15.4	16.5	27.8	9.9	12.0	27.5
M1/M3	1.45	1.38	1.27	1.26	1.23	1.14
M1 Total	349.5	354.9	363.3	371.3	278.4	382.6
Margin M1	6.1	5.4	8.4	8.0	7.1	4.2
M2 Total	980.6	1000.4	1011.9	1037.1	1060.9	1081.0
Margin M2	16.6	19.8	11.5	25.2	23.8	20.1
	Jul	Oct	Jan	Apr	Jul	Oct
Year			1979			

Daily Treasury Statements
Federal Reserve Statistical Releases

Year	1980				1981	
	Jan	Apr	Jul	Oct	Jan	Apr
Grand T	1826.4	1856.0	1906.3	1956.7	2023.5	2087.6
Margin	28.0	29.6	50.3	50.4	66.8	64.1
M3 Total	340.2	348.3	357.2	368.2	412.9	423.1
Margin M3	5.4	8.1	8.9	11.0	44.7	10.2
M1/M3	1.15	1.11	1.11	1.12	1.01	1.02
M1 Total	390.4	386.7	394.6	410.7	416.4	431.0
Margin M1	7.8	(3.7)	7.9	16.1	5.7	14.6
M2 Tota	1095.8	1121.1	1154.5	1177.8	1194.2	1233.5
Margin M2	14.8	25.2	33.5	23.3	16.4	39.3
	Jan	Apr	Jul	Oct	Jan	Apr
Year	1980				1981	

Daily Treasury Statements
Federal Reserve Statistical Releases

Year			1982			
	Jul	Oct	Jan	Apr	Jul	Oct
Grand T	2140.1	2209.5	2276.6	2328.1	2373.5	2441.8
Margin	52.5	69.4	67.1	51.5	45.4	68.3
M3 Total	455.0	483.1	503.8	520.2	535.7	561.1
Margin M3	31.9	28.1	20.7	16.4	15.5	25.4
M1/M3	0.94	0.89	0.89	0.87	0.84	0.83
M1 Total	427.7	429.7	448.4	451.1	449.5	465.7
Margin M1	(3.3)	2.0	18.7	2.7	(1.6)	16.2
M2 Tota	1257.4	1296.7	1324.4	1356.8	1388.3	1415.0
Margin M2	23.9	39.3	27.7	32.4	31.5	26.7
	Jul	Oct	Jan	Apr	Jul	Oct
Year			1982			

Daily Treasury Statements
Federal Reserve Statistical Releases

Year	1983				1984	
	Jan	Apr	Jul	Oct	Jan	Apr
Grand T	2492.3	2555.7	2597.6	2649.4	2721.4	2802.1
Margin	50.5	63.4	41.9	51.8	72.0	80.7
M3 Total	524.5	518.7	524.9	544.4	573.5	602.9
Margi M3	(36.1)	(5.8)	6.2	19.5	29.1	29.4
M1/M3	0.92	0.96	0.97	0.95	0.92	0.90
M1 Total	482.8	498.6	510.5	517.2	530.2	539.9
Margin M1	17.1	15.8	11.9	6.7	13.0	9.7
M2 Tota	1485.0	1538.4	1562.2	1587.8	1617.7	1659.3
Margin M2	70.0	53.4	23.8	25.6	29.9	41.6
	Jan	Apr	Jul	Oct	Jan	Apr
Year	1983				1984	

Daily Treasury Statements
Federal Reserve Statistical Releases

Year			1985			
	Jul	Oct	Jan	Apr	Jul	Oct
Grand T	2870.7	2932.3	3026.5	3062.5	3111.9	3166.9
Margin	68.6	61.6	94.2	36.0	49.4	55.0
M3 Total	639.4	669.3	683.3	679.3	673.6	697.0
Margin M3	36.5	29.9	14.0	(4.0)	(5.7)	23.4
M1/M3	0.85	0.81	0.82	0.85	0.88	0.87
M1 Total	943.3	542.2	561.1	575.1	592.0	605.3
Margin M1	3.4	(1.1)	18.9	14.0	16.9	13.3
M2 Tota	1688.0	1720.8	1782.1	1808.1	1846.3	1864.6
Margin M2	28.7	32.8	61.3	26.0	38.2	18.3
	Jul	Oct	Jan	Apr	Jul	Oct
Year			1985			

Daily Treasury Statements
Federal Reserve Statistical Releases

Year	1986				1987	
	Jan	Apr	Jul	Oct	Jan	Apr
Grand T	3243.0	3309.9	3381.2	3453.7	3536.0	3568.1
Margin	76.1	66.9	71.3	72.5	82.3	32.1
M3 Total	728.6	741.8	744.9	764.8	778.3	784.9
Margin M3	31.6	13.2	3.1	19.9	13.5	6.6
M1/M3	0.86	0.87	0.90	0.91	0.95	0.96
M1 Total	626.6	647.0	673.4	692.2	737.1	752.0
Margin M1	21.3	20.4	26.4	18.8	44.9	14.9
M2 Tota	1887.8	1921.1	1962.9	1996.7	2020.6	2031.2
Margin M2	23.2	33.3	41.8	33.8	23.9	10.6
	Jan	Apr	Jul	Oct	Jan	Apr
Year	1986				1987	

Daily Treasury Statements
Federal Reserve Statistical Releases

Year			1988			
	Jul	Oct	Jan	Apr	Jul	Oct
Grand T	3359.8	3665.6	3719.9	3796.0	3851.5	3888.4
Margin	31.7	65.8	54.3	76.1	55.5	36.9
M3 Total	810.4	850.0	857.7	865.5	892.3	920.2
Margin M3	25.5	39.6	7.7	7.8	26.8	27.9
M1/M3	0.92	0.89	0.89	0.90	0.88	0.85
M1 Total	746.2	753.2	764.2	777.9	785.5	780.8
Margin M1	(5.8)	7.0	11.0	13.7	7.6	(4.7)
M2 Tota	2043.2	2062.4	2098.0	2152.6	2173.7	2187.4
Margin M2	12.0	19.2	35.6	54.6	21.1	13.7
	Jul	Oct	Jan	Apr	Jul	Oct
Year			1988			

Daily Treasury Statements
Federal Reserve Statistical Releases

Year	1989				1990	
	Jan	Apr	Jul	Oct	Jan	Apr
Grand T	3944.3	3980.0	4016.6	4043.6	4091.5	4117.1
Margin	55.9	35.7	36.6	27.0	47.9	25.6
M3 Total	939.4	950.8	955.1	927.8	914.7	890.9
Margin M3	19.2	11.4	4.3	(27.3)	(13.1)	(23.8)
M1/M3	0.84	0.83	0.82	0.84	0.86	0.92
M1 Total	792.1	790.2	780.7	783.2	800.7	816.2
Margin M1	11.3	(1.9)	(9.5)	2.5	17.5	15.5
M2 Tota	2212.8	2239.0	2280.8	2332.6	2376.1	2410.0
Margin M2	25.4	26.2	41.8	51.8	43.5	33.9
	Jan	Apr	Jul	Oct	Jan	Apr
Year	1989				1990	

Daily Treasury Statements
Federal Reserve Statistical Releases

Year			1991			
	Jul	Oct	Jan	Apr	Jul	Oct
Grand T	4124.6	4148.9	4176.8	4219.6	4195.5	4185.4
Margin	7.5	24.3	27.9	42.8	(24.1)	(10.1)
M3 Total	894.6	889.3	880.6	862.3	833.9	824.7
Margin M3	3.7	(5.3)	(8.7)	(18.3)	(28.4)	(9.2)
M1/M3	0.91	0.92	0.94	0.99	1.03	1.06
M1 Total	811.0	816.1	831.7	851.9	860.9	874.0
Margin M1	(5.2)	5.1	15.6	20.2	9.0	13.1
M2 Tota	2419.0	2443.5	2464.5	2505.4	2500.7	2486.7
Margin M2	9.0	24.5	21.0	40.9	(4.7)	(14.9)
	Jul	Oct	Jan	Apr	Jul	Oct
Year			1991			

Daily Treasury Statements
Federal Reserve Statistical Releases

Year	1992				1993	
	Jan	Apr	Jul	Oct	Jan	Apr
Grand T	4216.1	4238.0	4209.8	4225.2	4207.2	4222.2
Margin	30.7	21.9	(28.2)	15.4	(18.0)	15.0
M3 Total	826.1	812.3	808.9	799.1	775.5	783.7
Margin M3	1.4	(13.8)	(3.4)	(9.8)	(23.6)	8.2
M1/M3	1.11	1.17	1.19	1.25	1.38	1.35
M1 Total	916.4	953.7	962.0	1000.8	1069.8	1057.4
Margin M1	42.4	37.3	8.3	38.8	69.0	(12.4)
M2 Tota	2473.6	2472.0	2438.9	2425.3	2361.9	2381.1
Margin M2	(13.1)	(1.6)	(33.1)	(13.6)	(63.4)	19.2
	Jan	Apr	Jul	Oct	Jan	Apr
Year	1992				1993	

Daily Treasury Statements
Federal Reserve Statistical Releases

Year			1994			
	Jul	Oct	Jan	Apr	Jul	Oct
Grand T	4231.4	4249.5	4284.7	4303.0	4313.3	4331.2
Margin	9.2	18.1	35.2	18.3	10.3	17.9
M3 Total	779.8	787.3	794.1	784.1	810.7	841.1
Margin M3	(3.9)	7.5	6.8	(10.0)	26.6	30.4
M1/M3	1.39	1.41	1.44	1.47	1.42	1.37
M1 Tota	1083.1	1111.6	1141.7	1152.2	1150.3	1147.7
Margin M1	25.7	28.5	30.1	10.5	(1.9)	(2.4)
M2 Tota	2368.5	2350.6	2348.9	2366.7	2362.3	2342.4
Margi M2	(12.6)	(17.9)	(1.7)	17.8	(14.4)	(9.9)

	Jul	Oct	Jan	Apr	Jul	Oct
Year			1994			

Daily Treasury Statements
Federal Reserve Statistical Releases

Year	1995				1996	
	Jan	Apr	Jul	Oct	Jan	Apr
Grand T	4392.8	4449.2	4532.5	4599.5	4670.8	4765.0
Margin	51.6	56.4	83.3	67.0	71.3	94.2
M3 Total	886.7	916.5	951.4	986.2	1008.1	1032.0
Margin M3	45.6	29.8	34.9	34.8	21.9	23.9
M1/M3	1.31	1.27	1.20	1.15	1.12	1.10
M1 Tota	1159.0	1159.9	1145.2	1132.4	1129.4	1131.1
Margin M1	11.3	0.9	(14.7)	(12.8)	(3.0)	1.7
M2 Tota	2347.1	2372.8	2435.9	2480.9	2533.3	2601.9
Margin M2	4.7	25.7	63.1	45.0	52.4	68.6
	Jan	Apr	Jul	Oct	Jan	Apr
Year	1995				1996	

Daily Treasury Statements
Federal Reserve Statistical Releases

Year			1997			
	Jul	Oct	Jan	Apr	Jul	Oct
Grand T	4821.6	4905.6	5014.6	5137.9	5208.6	5351.0
Margin	56.6	84.0	109.0	123.3	70.7	142.4
M3 Tota	1076.1	1137.6	1179.5	1235.8	1291.7	1375.7
Margin M3	44.1	61.5	41.9	56.3	55.9	84.0
M1/M3	1.03	0.95	0.92	0.87	0.83	0.77
M1 Tota	1110.0	1077.6	1086.3	1073.1	1065.3	1057.1
Margi M1	(21,1)	(32.4)	8.7	(13.2)	(7.8)	(8.2)
M2 Tota	2635.5	2690.4	2748.8	2829.0	2851.6	2918.2
Margin M2	33.6	54.9	58.4	80.2	22.6	66.6
	Jul	Oct	Jan	Apr	Jul	Oct
Year			1997			

Daily Treasury Statements
Federal Reserve Statistical Releases

Year	1998				1999	
	Jan	Apr	Jul	Oct	Jan	Apr
Grand T	5514.3	5671.9	5713.2	5918.9	6094.1	6202.9
Margin	163.3	157.6	41.3	205.7	175.2	108.8
M3 Tota	1451.8	1499.3	1519.0	1621.5	1676.9	1689.7
Margin M3	76.1	47.5	19.7	102.5	55.4	12.8
M1/M3	0.74	0.73	0.71	0.66	0.66	0.66
M1 Tota	1079.4	1086.9	1073.5	1076.1	1102.8	1112.5
Margin M1	22.3	7.5	(13.4)	2.6	26.7	9.7
M2 Tota	2983.1	3085.7	3120.7	3221.3	3314.4	3400.7
Margin M2	64.9	102.6	35.0	100.6	93.1	86.3
	Jan	Apr	Jul	Oct	Jan	Apr
Year	1998				1999	

Daily Treasury Statements
Federal Reserve Statistical Releases

Year			2000			
	Jul	Oct	Jan	Apr	Jul	Oct
Grand T	6223.4	6337.5	6620.7	6801.6	6828.3	6973.0
Margin	20.5	114.1	283.2	182.9	26.7	144.7
M3 Tota	1697.1	1755.7	1934.5	1986.1	2043.8	2108.3
Margin M3	7.4	58.6	178.8	51.6	57.7	64.5
M1/M3	0.65	0.62	0.58	0.57	0.54	0.52
M1 Tota	1096.3	1094.7	1126.3	1124.3	1103.2	1092.9
Margi M1	(16.2)	(1.6)	31.6	(2.0)	(21.1)	(10.3)
M2 Tota	3430.0	3487.1	3559.9	3691.2	3681.3	3771.8
Margin M2	29.3	57.1	72.8	131.3	(9.9)	90.5
	Jul	Oct	Jan	Apr	Jul	Oct
Year			2000			

Daily Treasury Statements
Federal Reserve Statistical Releases

Year	2001				2002	
	Jan	Apr	Jul	Oct	Jan	Apr
Grand T	7248.8	7529.2	7626.3	7824.0	8070.8	8155.8
Margin	275.8	280.4	97.1	197.7	246.8	85.0
M3 Tota	2256.0	2342.7	2421.8	2483.9	2597.2	2602.6
Margi M3	147.7	86.7	79.1	62.1	113.3	5.4
M1/M3	0.49	0.48	0.47	0.47	0.46	0.46
M1 Tota	1099.4	1122.2	1136.4	1156.2	1187.1	1190.4
Margin M1	6.5	22.8	14.2	19.8	30.9	3.3
M2 Tota	3893.4	4064.3	4068.1	4183.9	4286.5	4362.8
Margi M2	121.6	170.9	3.8	115.8	102.6	76.3
	Jan	Apr	Jul	Oct	Jan	Apr
Year	2001				2002	

Daily Treasury Statements
Federal Reserve Statistical Releases

Year			2003			
	Jul	Oct	Jan	Apr	Jul	Oct
Grand T	8184.4	8300.7	8578.2	8687.8	8814.1	8808.8
Margin	28.6	116.3	277.5	109.6	126.3	(5.3)
M3 Tota	2583.8	2591.6	2759.4	2725.7	2761.8	2747.7
Margi M3	(18.8)	7.8	167.8	(33.7)	36.1	(14.1)
M1/M3	0.46	0.46	0.44	0.46	0.46	0.46
M1 Tota	1195.0	1194.2	1222.0	1256.2	1274.3	1275.1
Margin M1	4.6	(0.8)	27.8	34.2	18.1	0.8
M2 Tota	4405.6	4514.9	4596.8	4705.9	4778.0	4786.0
Margin M2	42.8	109.3	81.9	109.1	72.1	8.0
	Jul	Oct	Jan	Apr	Jul	Oct
Year			2003			

Daily Treasury Statements
Federal Reserve Statistical Releases

Year	2004				2005	
	Jan	Apr	Jul	Oct	Jan	Apr
Grand T	8882.9	9104.1	9288.4	9375.8	9484.3	9620.7
Margin	74.1	221.2	184.3	87.4	108.5	136.4
M3 Tota	2829.4	2877.3	3003.3	3008.2	3042.1	3139.2
Margin M3	81.7	47.9	126.0	4.9	33.9	97.1
M1/M3	0.46	0.46	0.45	0.45	0.45	0.43
M1 Tota	1288.0	1330.8	1331.4	1353.9	1358.0	1361.0
Margin M1	12.9	42.8	0.6	22.5	4.1	3.0
M2 Tota	4765.5	4896.0	4953.7	5013.7	5084.2	5120.5
Margi M2	(20.5)	130.5	57.7	60.0	70.5	36.3
	Jan	Apr	Jul	Oct	Jan	Apr
Year	2004				2005	

Daily Treasury Statements
Federal Reserve Statistical Releases

Year			2006	
	Jul	Oct	Jan	Apr
Grand Tot	9776.8	10058.1	10217.7	??
Margin	156.1	281.3	159.6	??
M3 Total	3251.7	3430.9	3512.5	Discontinued March 2006
Margin M3	112.5	179.2	81.6	
M1/M3	0.42	0.40	0.39	
M1 Total	1354.3	1367.6	1377.3	1397.2
Margin M1	(6.7)	13.3	9.7	19.9
M2 Total	5170.8	5259.6	5327.9	5447.7
Margin M2	50.3	88.8	68.3	119.8
	Jul	Oct	Jan	Apr
Year			2006	

Daily Treasury Statements
Federal Reserve Statistical Releases

Appendix 3

Standards of Living From: NationsOnLine.org
Population From: Internet
December 12, 2014

		Standard of living	Population in millions
1	Timor-Leste South-East Asia	400	1.152
2	Malawi Eastern Africa	596	16.829
3	Somalia Eastern Africa	600	10.806
4	Democratic Republic of the Congo Middle Africa	675	67.514
5	Tanzania Eastern Africa	720	49.253
6	Yemen Middle East	745	24.407
7	Burundi Eastern Africa	753	10.163
8	Afghanistan Central Asia	800	31.853
9	Guinea-Bissau Western Africa	856	1.746
10	Ethiopia Eastern Africa	859	96.506
11	Niger Western Africa	896	17.831
12	Liberia Western Africa	900	4.517
13	Sierra Leone Western Africa	901	6.205
14	Madagascar Eastern Africa	911	23.572
15	Zambia Eastern Africa	911	15.021
16	Eritrea Eastern Africa	917	16.536
17	Mali Western Africa	1,084	15.804
18	Tuvalu Polynesia	1,100	.010
19	Kenya Africa	1,125	41.800
20	Benin Western Africa	1,147	10.323
21	Central African Republic Middle Africa	1,163	4.616
22	Nigeria Western Africa	1,188	180.768
23	Burkina Faso Western Africa	1,326	16.935
24	Mozambique Eastern Africa	1,335	26.713
25	Tajikistan Central Asia	1,373	8.371
26	Republic of the Congo Middle Africa	1,379	67.514
27	Korea (North) Eastern Asia	1,400	24.895
28	Myanmar (Burma) South-East Asia	1,417	53.259
29	Rwanda Eastern Africa	1,431	11.777
30	Nepal South-Central Asia	1,471	26.495

	Standard of living	Population in millions
31 Côte d'Ivoire West Africa	1,475	20.316
32 Togo Western Africa	1,600	6.817
33 Marshall Islands Micronesia	1,600	.054
34 Haiti Caribbean	1,614	10.317
35 São Tomé and Príncipe Middle Africa	1,638	.187
36 Comoros Eastern Africa	1,717	.735
37 Chad Middle Africa	1,744	12.825
38 Uganda Eastern Africa	1,817	36.824
39 Uzbekistan Central Asia	1,834	30.700
40 Senegal Western Africa	1,914	14.133
41 Solomon Islands Melanesia	1,922	.580
42 Djibouti Eastern Africa	1,957	.873
43 Guinea Western Africa	1,986	12.044
44 Bangladesh South-Central Asia	1,998	156.595
45 The Gambia Western Africa	1,999	1.839
46 Federated States of Micronesia	2,000	.104
47 Mongolia North-East Asia	2,046	2.839
48 Laos South-East Asia	2,049	6.770
49 Kyrgyzstan Central Asia	2,061	5.720
50 Cambodia South-East Asia	2,116	15.408
51 Lesotho Southern Africa	2,163	2.098
52 Moldova Eastern Europe	2,262	3.559
53 Cameroon Middle Africa	2,284	22.254
54 Mauritania North Western Africa	2,307	3.890
55 Zimbabwe South-Eastern Africa	2,413	14.150
56 Papua New Guinea Melanesia	2,414	7.321
57 Sudan North Africa	2,417	38.764
58 Pakistan Central Asia	2,567	182.590
59 Kiribati Micronesia	2,591	.104
60 Ghana Western Africa	2,601	25.905
61 Nicaragua Central America	2,779	6.080
62 Viet Nam South-East Asia	2,782	92.548
63 Honduras Central America	2,793	8.098
64 Angola Middle Africa	2,829	21.472
65 Cuba Caribbean	3,000	11.259
66 Georgia Western Asia	3,038	4.556
67 Bolivia South America	3,049	10.671
68 India South Asia	3,262	1,263.390
69 Bhutan South-Central Asia	3,330	.754
70 Vanuatu Melanesia	3,397	.253
71 Iraq Middle East	3,500	34.776

	Standard of living	Population in millions
72 Indonesia South-East Asia	3,853	252.812
73 Syria Middle East	3,871	21.987
74 Ecuador South America	4,010	15.738
75 Armenia Western Asia	4,048	2.977
76 Guatemala Central America	4,136	15.824
77 Sri Lanka South Asia	4,145	20.483

10% or less of the standard of living of the US
38.7% of the countries
45.4% of the population

78 Egypt North Africa	4,282	83.387
79 Morocco North Africa	4,444	32.853
80 Jamaica Caribbean	4,471	2.715
81 Azerbaijan Central Asia	4,500	9.417
82 El Salvador Central America	4,525	6.340
83 Jordan Middle East	4,615	7.505
84 Paraguay America	4,663	6.802
85 Guyana South America	4,685	.800
86 Philippines South-East Asia	4,770	100.876
87 Nauru Micronesia	5,000	.010
88 Swaziland Southern Africa	5,181	1.250
89 Serbia and Montenegro Southern Europe	5,204	7.164
90 Albania Southern Europe	5,323	2.774
91 Saint Lucia Caribbean	5,516	.182
92 Peru South America	5,594	30.376
93 Venezuela South America	5,801	30.425
94 Bosnia and Herzegovina Southern Europe	5,827	3.829
95 Réunion (French overseas) Eastern Africa	6,000	.871
96 Suriname South America	6,025	.549
97 China (Mainland) East Asia	6,193	1,397.498
98 Lebanon Middle East	6,205	4.467

15% or less of the standard of living of the US
49.2% of the countries
69.2% of the population

99 Dominica Caribbean	6,250	.072

189

		Standard of living	Population in millions
100	Fiji Melanesia	6,282	.881
101	Cape Verde Western Africa	6,287	.499
102	Samoa Polynesia	6,390	10.806
103	Namibia West-South Africa	6,658	2.105
104	Saint Vincent and the Grenadines Caribbean	6,679	.106
105	Gabon Middle Africa	6,977	1.672
106	Dominican Republic Caribbean	7,055	10.415
107	Algeria North Africa	7,095	39.208
108	Ukraine Eastern Europe	7,182	45.737
109	Colombia South America	7,303	48.321
110	Panama Central America	7,327	3.864
111	Belize Central America	7,635	.332
112	Maldives South Asia	7,640	.345
113	Tonga Polynesia	7,706	.105
114	Republic of Macedonia Southern Europe	7,749	2.071
115	Turkmenistan Central Asia	7,854	5.240
116	Turkey Europe/Asia	7,958	76.668
117	Iran Central Asia	8,065	77.447
118	Belarus Eastern Europe	8,186	9.464
119	Tunisia North Africa	8,223	10.887
120	Kazakhstan Central Asia	8,252	17.038
121	Romania Eastern Europe	8,258	19.964
122	French Guiana South America	8,300	.258

20% or less of the standard of living of the US
61.3% of the countries
74.5% of the population

		Standard of living	Population in millions
123	Thailand South-East Asia	8,542	67.223
124	Grenada Caribbean	8,608	.106
125	Brazil South America	8,745	202.034
126	Palau Micronesia	9,000	.021
127	Bulgaria Southern Europe	9,205	7.265
128	Uruguay South America	9,619	3.407
129	Mexico North America	10,090	124.469
130	Costa Rica Central America	10,316	4.872

25% or less of the standard of living of the US
65.3% of the countries
80.1% of the population

		Standard of living	Population in millions
131	Botswana Southern Africa	10,866	2.021
132	South Africa South Africa	11,035	53.140
133	Malaysia South-East Asia	11,160	30.188
134	Russian Federation Northern Asia	11,209	142.716
135	Libyan Arab Jamahiriya North Africa	11,354	6.202
136	Chile South America	11,537	17.620
137	Antigua and Barbuda Caribbean	11,604	.091
138	Seychelles Eastern Africa	12,135	.890
139	Croatia (Hrvatska) Southern Europe	12,364	4.281

30% or less of the standard of living of the US
69.8% of the countries
83.7% of the population

		Standard of living	Population in millions
140	Latvia Northern Europe	12,886	2.039
141	Mauritius Eastern Africa	13,029	1.296
142	Saudi Arabia Middle East	13,123	29.200
143	Argentina South America	13,153	41.446
144	Poland Eastern Europe	13,275	38.533
145	Trinidad and Tobago Caribbean	13,958	1.335
146	Lithuania Northern Europe	14,198	2.972
147	New Caledonia Melanesia	15,000	.260
148	Saint Kitts and Nevis Caribbean	15,050	.055
149	Slovakia Eastern Europe	16,110	5.411
150	Kuwait Middle East	16,297	3.369
151	Oman Middle East	16,300	3.314
152	Estonia Northern Europe	16,461	1.230

40% or less of the standard of living of the US
76.4% of the countries
85.5% of the population

		Standard of living	Population in millions
153	Hungary Eastern Europe	16,627	9.897
154	Barbados Caribbean	17,170	.287
155	French Polynesia Tahiti (France)	17,500	.280
156	Puerto Rico (USA) Caribbean	17,700	3.689
157	The Bahamas Caribbean	19,139	.377
158	Macau (China) Eastern Asia	19,400	.608
159	Czech Republic Eastern Europe	19,475	10.516
160	Bahrain Middle East	19,748	1.332

		Standard of living	Population in millions
161	Portugal Southern Europe	19,949	10.460
162	Malta Southern Europe	20,015	.423
163	Cyprus Europe/Asia	20,669	1.141

50% or less of the standard of living of the US
81.9% of the countries
86% of the population

		Standard of living	Population in millions
164	Greece Southern Europe	21,529	11.032
165	Slovenia Southern Europe	21,695	.059
166	South Korea East Asia	22,543	51.202
167	Israel Middle East	22,944	8.200
168	Equatorial Guinea Middle Africa	23,154	.757
169	United Arab Emirates Middle East	23,723	9.346
170	Netherlands Antilles Caribbean	23,770	.208
171	Spain Southern Europe	24,803	46.508
172	New Zealand Oceania	24,805	4.550
173	Brunei Darussalam South-East Asia	24,826	.416
174	Liechtenstein Western Europe	25,000	.037
175	Andorra Southern Europe	26,800	.080
176	Monaco Western Europe	27,000	.037
177	Taiwan (Republic of China) East Asia	27,122	23.374
178	Singapore South-East Asia	28,228	5.399
179	France Western Europe	29,203	66.821
180	Italy Southern Europe	29,414	61.070
181	Sweden Northern Europe	29,537	9.665
182	Qatar Middle East	29,607	2.268
183	Germany Western Europe	30,150	82.619
184	United Kingdom Northern Europe	30,309	64.097
185	Netherlands Western Europe	30,363	16.800
186	Finland Northern Europe	30,818	5.439
187	Australia Oceania	31,020	23.714
188	Japan East Asia	31,384	127.641
189	Belgium Western Europe	31,549	11.162

75% or less of the standard of living of the US
95% of the countries
94.7% of the population

		Standard of living	Population in millions
190	Hong Kong (China) Asia	32,292	7.188

		Standard of living	Population in millions
191	Austria Western Europe	32,962	8.484
192	Switzerland Western Europe	33,168	8.081
193	Canada North America	34,444	35.432
194	San Marino Southern Europe	34,600	.032
195	Denmark Northern Europe	34,718	5.591
196	Iceland Northern Europe	35,686	.333
197	Bermuda North America	36,000	.065
198	Ireland Northern Europe	40,003	4.595
199	United States North America	41,557	309.975
200	Norway Northern Europe	41,941	5.109
201	Luxembourg Western Europe	66,821	.525

Appendix 4

This is a chart of the national debt of the United States. The double x indicates years in which the debt was reduced.

Year	Total National Debt		Annual Change
1790	$75,463,476		
1791	$77,227,924		$1,764,448
1792	$80,358,634		$3,130,709
1793	$78,427,404	xx	($1,931,229)
1794	$80,747,587		$2,320,182
1795	$83,762,172		$3,014,584
1796	$82,064,479	xx	($1,697,692)
1797	$79,228,529	xx	($2,835,950)
1798	$78,408,669	xx	($819,859)
1799	$82,976,294		$4,567,624
1800	$83,038,050		$61,756
1801	$80,712,632	xx	($2,325,418)
1802	$77,054,686	xx	($3,657,946)
1803	$86,427,120		$9,372,434
1804	$82,312,150	xx	($4,114,970)
1805	$75,723,270	xx	($6,588,879)
1806	$69,218,398	xx	($6,504,872)
1807	$65,196,317	xx	($4,022,080)
1808	$57,023,190	xx	($8,173,125)
1809	$53,173,217	xx	($3,849,974)
1810	$48,005,587	xx	($5,167,629)
1811	$45,209,737	xx	($2,795,849)
1812	$55,962,827		$10,753,089
1813	$81,487,846		$25,525,018
1814	$99,833,660		$18,345,813
1815	$127,334,933		$27,501,273
1816	$123,491,965	xx	($3,842,968)
1817	$103,466,633	xx	($20,025,331)
1818	$95,529,648	xx	($7,936,985)
1819	$91,015,566	xx	($4,514,082)
1820	$89,987,427	xx	($1,028,138)

1821	$93,546,676		$3,559,249
1822	$90,875,877	xx	($2,670,799)
1823	$90,269,777	xx	($606,099)
1824	$83,788,432	xx	($6,481,345)
1825	$81,054,059	xx	($2,734,372)
1826	$73,987,357	xx	($7,066,702)
1827	$67,475,043	xx	($6,512,313)
1828	$58,421,413		$9,053,630
1829	$48,565,406	xx	($9,856,007)
1830	$39,123,191	xx	($9,442,214)
1831	$24,332,235	xx	($14,790,956)
1832	$7,001,698	xx	($17,330,536)
1833	$4,760,082	xx	($2,241,616)
1834	$33,733	xx	($4,726,349)
1835	$37,513		$3,780
1836	$336,957		$299,444
1837	$3,308,124		$2,971,166
1838	$10,434,221		$7,126,097
1839	$3,573,343	xx	($6,860,877)
1840	$5,250,875		$1,677,531
1841	$13,594,480		$8,343,605
1842	$32,742,922		$19,148,441
1843	$23,461,652	xx	($9,281,269)
1844	$15,925,303	xx	($7,536,349)
1845	$15,550,202	xx	($375,100)
1846	$38,826,534		$23,276,331
1847	$47,044,862		$8,218,327
1848	$63,061,858		$16,016,996
1849	$63,452,773		$390,914
1850	$68,304,796		$4,852,022
1851	$66,199,341	xx	($2,105,454)
1852	$59,803,117	xx	($6,396,224)
1853	$42,242,222	xx	($17,560,895)
1854	$35,586,956	xx	($6,655,265)
1855	$31,972,537	xx	($3,614,418)
1856	$28,699,831	xx	($3,272,706)
1857	$44,911,881		$16,212,049
1858	$58,496,837		$13,584,956
1859	$64,842,287		$6,345,450
1860	$90,580,873		$25,738,585

1861	$524,176,412		$433,595,538
1862	$1,119,772,138		$595,595,726
1863	$1,815,784,370		$696,012,231
1864	$2,680,647,869		$864,863,499
1865	$2,773,236,173		$92,588,303
1866	$2,678,126,103	xx	($95,110,069)
1867	$2,611,687,851	xx	($66,438,252)
1868	$2,588,452,213	xx	($23,235,637)
1869	$2,480,672,427	xx	($107,779,786)
1870	$2,353,211,332	xx	($127,461,095)
1871	$2,253,251,328	xx	($99,960,003)
1872	$2,234,482,993	xx	($18,768,335)
1873	$2,251,690,468		$17,207,475
1874	$2,232,284,531	xx	($19,405,936)
1875	$2,180,395,067	xx	($51,889,464)
1876	$2,205,301,392		$24,906,324
1877	$2,256,205,892		$50,904,500
1878	$2,349,567,482	xx	($93,361,589)
1879	$2,120,415,370	xx	($229,152,111)
1880	$2,069,013,569	xx	($51,401,801)
1881	$1,918,312,994	xx	$150,700,575)
1882	$1,884,171,728	xx	($34,141,265)
1883	$1,830,528,923	xx	($53,642,804)
1884	$1,863,964,873		$33,435,949
1885	$1,775,063,013	xx	($88,901,859)
1886	$1,657,602,592	xx	($117,460,421)
1887	$1,692,858,984		$35,256,391
1888	$1,619,052,922	xx	($73,806,062)
1889	$1,552,140,204	xx	($66,912,717)
1890	$1,545,996,591	xx	($6,143,613)
1891	$1,588,464,144		$42,467,553
1892	$1,545,985,686	xx	($42,478,458)
1893	$1,632,253,636		$86,267,950
1894	$1,676,120,983		$43,867,346
1895	$1,769,840,323		$93,719,340
1896	$1,817,672,665		$47,832,342
1897	$1,796,531,995	xx	($21,140,670)
1898	$1,991,927,306		$195,395,311
1899	$2,136,961,091		$145,033,784
1900	$2,143,326,933		$6,365,842

197

Year		
1901	$2,158,610,445	$15,283,512
1902	$2,202,464,781	$43,854,336
1903	$2,264,003,585	$61,538,803
1904	$2,274,615,063	$10,611,478
1905	$2,337,161,839	$62,546,775
1906	$2,457,188,061	$120,026,222
1907	$2,626,806,271	$169,618,210
1908	$2,639,546,241	$12,739,969
1909	$2,652,665,838	$13,119,597
1910	$2,765,600,606	$112,934,768
1911	$2,868,373,874	$102,773,267
1912	$2,916,204,913	$47,831,039
1913	$2,912,499,269 xx	($3,705,644)
1914	$3,058,136,873	$145,637,604
1915	$3,609,244,262	$551,107,389
1916	$5,717,770,279	$2,108,526,017
1917	$14,592,161,414	$8,874,391,134
1918	$27,390,970,113	$12,798,808,699
1919	$25,952,456,406 xx	($1,438,513,706)
1920	$23,977,450,552 xx	($1,975,005,853)
1921	$22,963,381,708 xx	($1,014,068,844)
1922	$22,349,707,365 xx	($613,674,342)
1923	$21,250,812,989 xx	($1,098,894,375)
1924	$20,516,193,887 xx	($734,619,101)
1925	$19,643,216,315 xx	($872,977,572)
1926	$18,511,906,931 xx	($1,131,309,383)
1927	$17,604,293,201 xx	($907,613,730)
1928	$16,931,088,484 xx	($673,204,717)
1929	$16,185,309,831 xx	($745,778,652)
1930	$16,801,281,491	$615,971,660
1931	$19,487,002,444	$2,685,720,952
1932	$22,538,672,560	$3,051,670,116
1933	$27,053,141,414	$4,514,468,854
1934	$28,700,892,224	$1,647,750,810
1935	$33,778,543,496	$5,077,651,272
1936	$36,424,613,732	$2,646,070,235
1937	$37,164,740,315	$740,126,583
1938	$40,439,532,411	$3,274,792,095
1939	$42,967,531,037	$2,527,998,626
1940	$48,961,443,535	$5,993,912,498

198

1941	$72,422,445,116		$23,461,001,580
1942	$136,696,090,320		$64,273,645,213
1943	$201,003,387,221		$64,307,296,891
1944	$258,682,187,409		$57,678,800,188
1945	$269,422,099,173		$10,739,911,763
1946	$258,286,383,108	xx	($11,135,716,064)
1947	$252,292,246,512	xx	($5,994,136,595)
1948	$252,770,359,860		$478,113,347
1949	$257,357,352,351		$4,586,992,490
1950	$255,221,976,814	xx	($2,135,375,536)
1951	$259,105,178,785		$3,883,201,970
1952	$266,071,061,638		$6,965,882,853
1953	$271,259,599,108		$5,188,537,469
1954	$274,374,222,802		$3,114,623,694
1955	$272,750,813,649	xx	($1,623,409,153)
1956	$270,527,171,896	xx	($2,223,641,752)
1957	$276,343,217,745		$5,816,045,849
1958	$284,705,907,078		$8,362,689,332
1959	$286,330,760,848		$1,624,853,770
1960	$288,970,938,610		$2,640,177,761
1961	$298,200,822,720		$9,229,884,110
1962	$305,859,632,996		$7,658,810,275
1963	$311,712,899,237		$5,853,266,240
1964	$317,273,898,983		$5,560,999,746
1965	$319,907,087,795		$2,633,188,811
1966	$326,220,937,794		$6,313,849,999
1967	$347,578,406,425		$21,357,468,631
1968	$353,720,253,841		$6,141,847,415
1968	$370,918,706,949		$17,198,453,108
1970	$398,129,744,455		$27,211,037,505
1971	$427,260,460,940		$29,130,716,484
1972	$458,141,605,312		$30,881,144,371
1973	$475,059,815,731		$16,918,210,419
1974	$533,189,000,000		$58,129,184,268
1975	$620,433,000,000		$87,244,000,000
1976	$698,840,000,000		$78,407,000,000
1977	$771,544,000,000		$72,704,000,000
1978	$826,519,000,000		$54,975,000,000
1979	$907,701,000,000		$81,182,000,000
1980	$997,855,000,000		$90,154,000,000

1981	$1,142,034,000,000	$144,179,000,000
1982	$1,377,210,000,000	$235,176,000,000
1983	$1,572,266,000,000	$195,056,000,000
1984	$1,823,103,000,000	$250,837,000,000
1985	$2,125,302,616,658	$302,199,616,658
1986	$2,350,276,890,953	$224,974,274,294
1987	$2,602,337,712,041	$252,060,821,088
1988	$2,857,430,960,187	$255,093,248,146
1989	$3,233,313,451,777	$375,882,491,589
1990	$3,665,303,351,697	$431,989,899,919
1991	$4,064,620,655,521	$399,317,303,824
1992	$4,411,488,883,139	$346,868,227,617
1993	$4,692,749,910,013	$281,261,026,873
1994	$4,973,982,900,709	$281,232,990,696
1995	$5,224,810,939,135	$250,828,038,426
1996	$5,413,146,011,397	$188,335,072,261
1997	$5,526,193,008,897	$113,046,997,500
1998	$5,656,270,901,615	$130,077,892,717
1999	$5,674,178,209,886	$17,907,308,271
2000	$5,807,463,412,200	$133,285,202,313
2001	$6,228,235,965,597	$420,772,553,397
2002	$6,783,231,062,743	$554,995,097,146
2003	$7,379,052,696,330	$595,821,633,586
2004	$7,932,709,661,723	$553,656,965,393
2005	$8,506,973,899,215	$574,264,237,491
2006	$9,007,653,372,262	$500,679,473,047
2007	$10,024,724,896,912	$1,017,071,524,650
2008	$11,909,829,003,511	$1,885,104,106,599
2009	$13,561,623,030,891	$1,651,794,027,380
2010	$14,790,340,328,557	$1,228,717,297,665
2011	$16,066,241,407,385	$1,275,901,078,828
2012	$16,738,183,526,697	$671,942,119,311
2013	$17,824,071,380,733	$1,085,887,854,036
2014	$18,150,617,666,484	$326,546,285,750
2015	$18,825,061,664,536	$674,443,998,051
2016	$19,864,000,000,000	$1,038,938,335,464
2017	$19,976,826,951,047	$112,826,951,047
2018	$20,597,795,000,000	$620,968,048,953

Appendix 5

DVD on Economics

These subjects on 1 DVD are available from the publisher.

1. Border Tax
2. Cash-Less Society
3. End Capitalism
4. FDIC
5. National Debt
6. Socialism
7. Student Debt
8. Understanding Derivatives
9. What is Inflation?
10. Who Prints our Money?

APPENDIX 6

Appendix 6 is a variation of the game of Monopoly, Trademark by Parker Brothers', showing how the Federal Reserve with its constant creation of money and the subsequent inflation has affected our standard of living. Try it and see what inflation caused by an increase in the money supply really looks like.

Monopoly – Federal Reserve/Central Bank

The usual Monopoly Game can be adjusted to form a new version that shows how the Federal Reserve/central bank works in the real world and how these actions affect us. This version shows the economic principles behind the Federal Reserve/central bank and how the creation of money and inflation operate. As an interesting sideline the current money we use here in the United States has no backing whatsoever and is considered fiat money, that is money that is just printed on paper with no real backing or value. The reason it has value is because the federal government decrees that it does. If the federal government decreed that the Monopoly money had value, it would!

New Monopoly sets usually have $16,550 total printed money. As a first step remove 11 of the $500 bills and 1 of the $50 bills and place them in the reserve fund. There will be two funds that must be kept separate: the reserve fund and the circulation fund. For ease of understanding the circulation fund will be held by the bank and the reserve fund will be held by the central bank. The circulation fund is used to pay the players and operate as the game progresses. The reserve fund is used to replenish the circulation fund when it runs out of money. The total money supply will start at $11,000. We will base all future creation of money on this amount to make the illustration easy to see.

Starting Money in the Circulation

40	$1 bills	40	$10 bills	22	$50 bills
40	$5 bills	48	$20 bills	23	$100 bills
		12	$500 bills		

Next using small paper sheets create, just like a central bank does, 10 bills of $10,000 each, 10 bills of $5,000 each, 20 bills of $1,000 each, and 20 bills of $100 each for a total of $172,000 of additional cash. This money is placed in the central bank/reserve fund and will be put into play as needed just as a central bank does. Here are two of the major functions of a central bank. Not only do they monitor the money in circulation, but they also hold hundreds of millions of dollars in reserve to circulate whenever they want to.

Remember, the central bank can create as much money as it wants for any reason. For purposes of the game just don't add it into circulation except as indicated in Rule # 3.

As the game is played, notice that as the first multiples of inflation occur the pain is very slight causing only a little twitch. Later the rents and the prices become a real burden demonstrating the real insidiousness of money creation and the inflation that follows. Also note how property grows in value through inflation. Is it any wonder then, that the very wealthy keep a lot of their money in real estate? This is also an indication of what we should aim for. It is also interesting that profits realized by the sale of real estate are not taxed if you immediately repurchase additional real estate of equal or higher value. Convenient for those of great wealth isn't it. Just look around, who really owns almost all of the real estate? Who controls those tax laws?

This version of the game not only demonstrates the function of the central bank for the wealthy, but it also shows how inflation directly affects us. Notice how the rents and prices of everything constantly increase as money is added. Now it is obvious that the rules of the game say that it will, but the rules are based on a fundamental economic formula $MV=PT$. M = money supply; V = velocity of the money through the economy; P = price; and T = the transactions in the economy. If, for purposes of illustration, V and T are held at 1, then it is easily seen how any increase in the money supply will directly affect the prices. Also don't forget a decrease in the money supply will also effect the prices. To help hide what is really happening, the Federal Reserve constantly draws attention to the interest rate. They regularly raise it and tell us it is to control inflation. In reality, if they would stop printing money they wouldn't need to raise the interest rate and THAT WOULD BE BETTER FOR US.

The game works easier if the number of players is limited to no more than six. Also try to have at least three.

The following are the adjusted rules for this version:

1. As the game progresses make all regular payments to the bank. When purchasing properties, hotels, houses, and

making interest payments place those in the central bank/reserve fund. If needed, this money can be used to make change to keep the small bills in circulation. In real life it wouldn't happen like this but it moves the game along and allows us to see the concept more quickly. (A variation would be to put the money in the center of the board and whenever players land on "Free Parking" they would collect it. I don't recommend this as in this case the game could continue forever and the inflation multiples would grow and grow much like the actual United States economy ever since the Federal Reserve took over.)

2. One of the players will be the banker. This player will have three functions. He will represent a normal player and also represent the bank and secretly he will represent the Federal Reserve/central bank. If as a normal player he runs out of money the bank will secretly provide him with needed funds. For the purposes of the game do not take this money from the central bank/reserve fund. Use the circulation fund so we do not introduce additional money before the right time.

3. Eventually the circulation fund will run out of money. When that happens the Federal Reserve/central bank will reach into its reserves and place an additional $11,000 into play from the reserve fund. The central bank will do this every time the circulation fund runs out of money. As the game progresses the circulation fund will run out of money faster. This demonstrates one of the actions of inflation. New money must be added faster and faster.

4. Each time new money is placed into circulation the prices will increase correspondingly. For example, when the

first $11,000 is put into play all costs, bonuses, prices, interest payments, rents, prices for properties, mortgage amounts, everything will all be multiplied by 2. The only exception will be the payment for going around "GO," that will remain at $200. Again, this is just to speed up the game. In the real world it would also double.

5. The next time $11,000 is added everything will increase by 3 times the original price. It continues in this pattern each time more money is placed into circulation. To make it easier to keep track of the inflation level, keep a piece of paper handy and make a mark each time money is added. A chart with the converted inflationary prices is provided. When using the conversion chart, first see what the original amount was and then follow the chart to the level of the inflation multiple, then apply any other factors.

6. When an individual goes bankrupt the bank will receive all mortgaged properties just as in real life. Now the bank has two options: 1. If the player representing the bank needs or even wants the property it is provided to that player and he then pays the mortgage amount. If the player doesn't have the money to pay the mortgage, then the bank will provide it under the table. 2. If there is no need or desire for that property the bank sells it to any player for the value of the mortgage or more if they want to pay it. The mortgage values will be at the current inflation level even if the property had been originally mortgaged at a lower level.

7. When a player goes bankrupt all cash and any properties that have not been mortgaged revert to the player causing the bankruptcy.

8. The "Income Tax" space is always $200 or the applicable multiple. It is never 10% of assets.

9. If a player goes bankrupt because of a requirement of a space on the board or based on a Community Chest or a Chance Card, then its money and all properties go to the bank. The bank pays all the remaining obligations of the transaction. Then it will treat the assets as specified in item #6.

10. When reselling a house or a hotel back to the bank there is a 10% cost in place of the regular 50% cost. The resell price will be based on the current inflation level.

Note: A Strategy - Assume that the player representing the bank has a great run of luck and at the beginning of the game acquires 17 to 18 of the properties including both Utilities, three Railroads, and the Boardwalk monopoly. While doing this he mortgages all of his properties. The opposite player perhaps has the New York monopoly and has been able to build it up to hotels.

Now the banker player has no money and therefore cannot build on its monopoly because every time it gets any money the money will go the other player and the game will continue in its current state as the inflation levels go up and up and all of the new money goes to the opposite player even though he has the worst position.

To overcome this the banker player appeals to the central bank/reserve fund for a bailout. The negotiations could conclude with a loan, not to be repaid and carrying no interest, of enough money to get all properties out of mortgage and a continuing line of credit any time a property will have to be mortgaged. The loan could even include enough money to build the hotels on Boardwalk at the current inflated price. When this occurs the difference between the loan and $11,000 would be placed in the circulation fund and another multiple would be added. This entire procedure would be justified by the idea that if this player went under it would be such a setback it would hurt the economy as a whole.

FINAL NOTE: YOU'RE RIGHT THE GAME ISN'T FAIR!!
THE BANK ALWAYS WINS!!!
BUT THEN THIS IS HOW THE WORLD
CENTRAL BANKING GAME IS REALLY PLAYED

INFLATION CONVERSION CHART

INFLATION LEVELS

Item or Dollar Amount	1	2	3	4	5	6	7	8	9
	2	4	6	8	10	12	14	16	18
	4	8	12	16	20	24	28	32	36
	6	12	18	24	30	36	42	48	54
	8	16	24	32	40	48	56	64	72
	10	20	30	40	50	60	70	80	90
	12	24	36	48	60	72	84	96	108
	14	28	42	56	70	84	98	112	126
	16	32	48	64	80	96	112	128	144
	18	36	54	72	90	108	126	144	162
	20	40	60	80	100	120	140	160	180
	22	44	66	88	110	132	154	176	198
	24	48	72	96	120	144	168	192	216
	26	52	78	104	130	156	182	208	234
	28	56	84	112	140	168	196	224	252
	35	70	105	140	175	210	245	280	315
	50	100	150	200	250	300	350	400	450
Income Tax	200	400	600	800	1000	1200	1400	1600	1800
Railroad	25	50	75	100	125	150	175	200	225
	50	100	150	200	250	300	350	400	450
	100	200	300	400	500	600	700	800	900
	200	400	600	800	1000	1200	1400	1600	1800
Luxury Tax	75	150	225	300	375	450	525	600	675
Electric &	X 4	X 8	X 12	X 16	X 20	X 24	X 28	X 32	X 36
Water Works	X 10	X 20	X 30	X 40	X 50	X 60	X 70	X 80	X 90

In the case of houses and hotels just multiply the rent times the inflation level.

In the case of bonuses or penalties from the Community Chest or Chance cards just multiply by the inflation level.

In the case of interest: First compute the interest amount and then multiply by the inflation level.

Index

A

B

compound interest - 53, 77, 78
confidence - 55, 67, 72, 115
confident - 16, 56
Congress - 15, 47, 48, 54, 61, 62, 69, 70, 79, 89, 95, 100, 104
congressmen - 61, 116
Constitution - 16, 54, 61, 79, 95, 97, 98, 100, 112, 118, 127
consulates - 96
consumers - 25, 48, 104
control - 5, 23, 24, 29, 30, 31, 32, 40, 60, 61, 68, 69, 71, 79, 81, 85, 92, 97, 100, 108, 112, 116, 117, 118, 120, 122, 125
controlled - 24, 30, 39, 50, 63, 69, 71, 108, 120, 122
controller - 39
controlling - 122
conversion chart - 207, 210
Costa Rica - 105
cost - 10, 11, 25, 32, 48, 49, 50, 56, 78, 91, 92, 95, 96, 99, 102, 112
Council on Foreign Relations (CFR) - 119
counterfeiters - 115
cow - 53
crazy - 117
creation of money - 17, 70, 203, 204
creation of value - 107, 110
credit cards - 56, 137
crook - 28
crops - 48
Cuba - 12, 118

D

Darussalam - 105

Du Pont - 11
Dutch East Indies - 132
duties - 15, 95, 96, 100
DVD - 201

E

earn - 7, 18, 19, 20, 34, 77, 78, 87, 91, 94, 98, 101
earners - 19, 20
earnings - 7
Eastern Seaboard - 136
econometrics - 59
economic formula - 58, 205
economic growth - 19, 85, 97
economic laws - 39, 57, 99, 107, 121
economic principles - 203
economic stimulus packages - 18
economic system - 23, 24, 108
economics - 5, 7, 9, 11, 12, 13, 18, 29, 30, 37, 39, 41, 51, 53,
56, 57, 58, 60, 69, 81, 82, 83, 84, 85, 88, 91, 93, 95, 96, 97,
99, 100, 108, 109, 110, 120, 121, 127, 201, 241
economies - 83, 85, 119, 120
economist - 10, 18, 30, 83, 84, 87, 100
education - 60, 93, 241
educators - 90
El Salvador - 105
elastic - 12, 41
elasticity - 13, 40, 41
end capitalism - 121, 122, 201
England - 118, 119
entry level jobs - 92
equalizer - 120

G

garbage - 18, 81
gas station attendants - 92
gasoline - 86
general welfare - 15, 95
geography - 32, 107
German - 11
Germany - 68, 95
give - 11, 27, 28, 30, 31, 32, 34, 69, 92, 94, 124
glass - 85, 86, 87
Gliberhaven - 65, 66, 67
global trade - 104
God - 133, 134
gold - 54, 61, 62
gold mine - 79
gold repository - 61
goldsmith - 65, 66
gold standard - 61, 63, 241
gold supply - 62
golf course - 87
goods - 9, 15, 17, 24, 29, 33, 56, 57, 88, 95, 96, 97, 102, 104, 108, 109, 133, 137
gouging laws - 49
government - 11, 12, 15, 16, 17, 18, 19, 20, 23, 24, 27, 28, 29, 31, 32, 33, 34, 35, 39, 40, 48, 49, 50, 51, 54, 56, 57, 61, 68, 70, 72, 75, 81, 82, 84, 85, 87, 88, 89, 90, 91, 92, 93, 94, 95, 96, 97, 99, 100, 103, 108, 112, 113, 114, 115, 116, 117, 118, 119, 120, 122, 124, 125, 127, 134, 135, 136, 241
government agencies - 33, 49
government control - 30, 40
government debt - 33, 34, 113
government dole - 94

I

I, Pencil - 39, 127, 128, 134, 135, 136
idle deposits - 66
idleness - 94
illegal - 61, 79
Illuminati - 60, 117
import - 15, 16, 95, 97, 100
import fees - 95
import taxes - 95
imposts - 15, 95, 100
inadequate aggregate demand - 81, 82
income - 16, 18, 19, 20, 66, 92, 93, 98
income tax - 16, 18, 20, 31, 208, 210
individual - 5, 10, 15, 23, 37, 48, 61, 65, 66, 68, 78, 79, 84,
89, 91, 94, 110, 115, 120, 122, 123, 124, 129, 135
Indonesia - 132
industries - 95, 96, 97, 102, 103, 107
industry - 19, 102
inelastic - 13, 41
in-elasticity - 12, 13, 40
inflation - 17, 18, 32, 33, 51, 54, 55, 57, 58, 59, 60, 68, 71,
74, 108, 114, 125, 137, 201, 203, 205, 206, 207, 208, 210,
241
inflationary - 58, 74, 107
insurable - 73
insurance - 72, 73, 74, 118
intellectual skills - 104
interest (dealing with money) - 18, 34, 53, 58, 60, 61, 66, 68,
70, 77, 78, 88, 111, 115, 116, 206, 207
interest rates - 7, 58, 60, 69, 205, 208, 210, 241
international - 12, 33, 61, 62, 96, 241

222

L

M

most favored nation trading status - 104
murder by government - 118
MV=PT - 58, 205

N

nation - 5, 16, 30, 85,104, 108, 114
national - 12, 113
national debt - 111, 112, 113, 114, 115, 195, 201
needs - 13, 14, 25, 74, 82, 92, 133
New World Order - 61, 89
New York - 136
New Zealand - 105
Nicaragua - 105
nitrates - 11
Nixon, Richard – President - 51, 62
non-debt debt - 116
North American Free Trade Agreement (NAFTA) - 104
Northern states - 99
Northwestern part of Europe - 98
not insurable - 73

O

Oakland, CA - 93
oath of office - 79
Obama, Barack – President - 114
Obamacare - 118
obsolete - 25
oil - 33, 131, 132, 133, 136

Oman - 105
opportunity - 11, 19, 20, 32, 66, 67, 92, 97, 124, 127
Oregon - 129, 132
organized crime - 35
other peoples' money - 119
output - 25

P

P - 59, 205
Pacific - 97, 105
Pacific Gas & Electric Company - 130
Panama - 105
parents - 90, 94, 130
pay - 10, 11, 15, 18, 19, 20, 25, 27, 28, 31, 32, 33, 34, 47,
48, 49, 60, 67, 68, 72, 78, 85, 88, 89, 91, 92, 93, 94, 95, 99,
101, 102, 103, 115, 118, 119, 121
peace - 15
pencil - 39, 40, 127, 128, 129, 130, 132, 133, 135
people - 7, 9, 11, 13, 15, 16, 20, 23, 25, 30, 31, 32, 34, 39,
41, 47, 48, 49, 50, 51, 53, 54, 55, 56, 57, 59, 60, 61, 67, 68,
70, 72, 79, 82, 83, 84, 85, 86, 87, 88, 89, 91, 92, 93, 94, 98,
99, 100, 101, 102, 103, 104, 107, 109, 112, 114, 115, 117,
118, 119, 121, 122, 123, 124, 129, 135
percentage - 18, 20, 113
Persian Gulf - 136
person - 18, 27, 28, 29, 31, 39, 72, 107, 117, 118, 121, 122,
123, 128, 129, 131, 132, 133, 136
personal debt - 113
personal property - 29, 30
Peru - 105
philosophy - 27

plane - 10
planned society - 40
plywood - 49, 50
political parties - 111, 114
politicians - 5, 7, 50, 60, 93, 105, 111
poor - 19, 96, 120, 124
population - 20, 48, 74, 90, 94, 99, 100, 101, 107, 108, 109
Powell, Jim - 12
power - 15, 23, 34, 59, 60, 61, 62, 69, 89, 95, 117
practical economics - 41, 241
prepay - 78
presidential - 34
price - 10, 16, 25, 33, 34, 39, 41, 42, 43, 44, 45, 46, 47, 48,
49, 50, 55, 56, 57, 59, 62, 90, 103
prices - 7, 12, 17, 25, 33, 34, 48, 49, 50, 51, 54, 56, 57, 58,
59, 68, 91, 92, 96, 97, 99, 102, 103, 104, 107, 108, 109, 137,
204, 205, 206, 207, 208, 209
principal - 77, 115
principles - 7, 9, 18, 33, 39, 83, 84, 85
printing of money - 57, 68, 73
prints - 37, 56, 57, 68, 69, 74, 128, 201
private company - 11, 118
private property - 15, 21, 24, 27, 29, 30, 31, 32, 38, 122
produce - 10, 11, 15, 19, 24, 25, 27, 47, 57, 86, 96, 100, 101,
102, 103, 107, 122, 123, 128, 241
producer - 10, 50, 103
production - 16, 17, 20, 25, 27, 29, 33, 39, 40, 48, 50, 54, 85,
87, 91, 103, 105, 127
product - 10, 25, 29, 40, 49, 50, 55, 57, 77, 91, 101, 102, 103,
104, 107, 109, 123, 131, 132
profit - 10, 19, 25, 60, 70, 84, 97, 116
profitable - 66, 67, 96, 103
profits - 10, 11, 16, 32, 37, 50, 60, 61, 69, 70, 72, 79, 91

progressive tax - 18, 19, 20
property - 15, 24, 27, 29, 30, 31, 32, 38, 204, 207, 209
property tax - 31
prosperity - 16, 17, 20, 104, 109, 110
provide - 15, 16, 18, 25, 27, 40, 69, 72, 73, 78, 81, 84, 85, 88, 89, 95, 97, 100, 116, 121, 123, 124, 125, 241
Provis Institute of Political Economics - 241
public schools - 114

Q

quagmire - 90

R

railroad - 48, 129
railroads - 208
random - 73
Read, Leonard - 39, 127
Reagan, Ronald – President - 17, 104
real estate - 205
real growth - 107
real property - 29, 30
real world - 18
receipts - 65
recession - 17, 54, 55, 71, 72, 81
redistribute - 31, 32
regressive tax - 19, 20
regulations - 32, 54, 85
rent - 204, 205, 207

S

W

Z

1

2

6

$6,000 - 93
6.25% - 113
68.3% - 113

8

8,000 - 84
$8,000 - 82

9

93.75% - 113

About the Author

He has been actively engaged in Economics for fifty-eight years with an Undergraduate degree in 1965 and a Master's degree in 1972. He completed his Doctorate in Political Economics in 2016. In the late 1960s he observed the creation of the two-tiered international gold standard resulting in the abolishment of the international gold standard in 1971. He then also observed the follow-on interest rate and inflation explosion of the 1970s.

He has followed the shadow government since the 1960s and has read hundreds of thousands of pages concerning politics and economics and their relationships over these fifty-five years. He began writing in 2005 and produced a political newsletter every Tuesday for six years, from 2006 to 2012.

He has completed a six volume set, *Liberty: Will it Survive the 21st Century,* comprising over 2,200 pages. The set presents the problems of government in our current society along with solutions.

He began The Provis Institute of Political Economics in January 2016 to award graduate degrees in Economics. This institute was established to provide an avenue for students to achieve an education within their financial capabilities that teaches practical economics for everyday life. The website can be found at ProvisInstitute.com.